T0323797

Stay Interesting

STAY INTERESTING

I Don't Always Tell Stories About My Life,
but When I Do They're True and Amazing

Jonathan Goldsmith

with Geoffrey Gray

DUTTON

DUTTON

An imprint of Penguin Random House LLC
1745 Broadway
New York, NY 10019
penguinrandomhouse.com

Copyright © 2017 by Jonathan Goldsmith
Penguin Random House values and supports copyright. Copyright fuels creativity,
encourages diverse voices, promotes free speech and creates a vibrant culture. Thank you
for buying an authorized edition of this book and for complying with copyright laws by not
reproducing, scanning, or distributing any part of it in any form without permission. You
are supporting writers and allowing Penguin Random House to continue to publish books
for every reader. Please note that no part of this book may be used or reproduced in any
manner for the purpose of training artificial intelligence technologies or systems.

DUTTON is a registered trademark and the D colophon
is a trademark of Penguin Random House LLC.

The photographs on pages ii, 1, 117, and 227 are courtesy of the author.

LIBRARY OF CONGRESS CATALOGING-IN-PUBLICATION DATA
has been applied for.

Hardcover ISBN 9781101986233
eBook ISBN 9781101986257
Paperback ISBN 9781101986240

Set in Dante MT Pro
Designed by Amy Hill

While the author has made every effort to provide accurate telephone numbers, Internet
addresses, and other contact information at the time of publication, neither
the publisher nor the author assumes any responsibility for errors or for changes that occur
after publication. Further, the publisher does not have any control over and does not
assume any responsibility for author or third-party websites or their content.

Penguin is committed to publishing works of quality and integrity.
In that spirit, we are proud to offer this book to our readers;
however, the story, the experiences, and the words
are the author's alone.

The authorized representative in the EU for product safety and compliance is
Penguin Random House Ireland, Morrison Chambers, 32 Nassau Street, Dublin D02 YH68,
Ireland, https://eu-contact.penguin.ie.

149927040

To my father, Milton, who taught me how to live
To my wife, Barbara, who taught me how to love
And to my children, for the ongoing inspiration

Contents

CONTENTS

Act II

CONTENTS

Act III

Finale

Stay Interesting

Act I

I woke up in the back of my truck and looked around the campground. It was empty. It was late fall and the backpackers and tourists who pass through Sycamore Canyon, which overlooks parts of Malibu on the California coast, were all gone. Even the folks who ran the campground had disappeared. I put on my sandals and walked over to the changing station to take a shower. Inside the drafty bathroom, which resembled the men's room at Mule Creek State Prison, I made my way to the showers, turned the lever, and waited on the cold cement floor in bare feet for the hot water to kick in. It never came.

Shit, I thought. What luck. A big audition today, my first in months, and I couldn't even take a hot shower. I was tired, having not slept well the night before, and doubts nagged me. Had I lost the ability to make people laugh in my ten years away from acting? Did I still have the charm, if I ever had it at all? So many years, so many almosts. Could I hide the bitterness? Could I stand another rejection? A whole lifetime of disappointments. I didn't want to go, but I didn't want to run away either.

From the back of my truck, I was reminded of how far I had fallen. The colony across the highway was buzzing. The moguls left their beautiful homes and beautiful wives and beautiful children and drove their beautiful sports cars to the studios. They had everything I wanted. In the distance, I could see the glow in the sky from the incredible houses overlooking the surf in the hills of Malibu. I could hear the sound of the ocean waves crashing as I imagined the lives of the people in those houses. Accomplished people. I felt totally isolated and ineffectual. I was living a nightmare that I used to have as a child, where somebody's fighting me and I can't move my shoulders or arms. Nothing works. I'm defenseless.

I'd been feeling that way a lot, given my downward trajectory. What had happened to me? How had I reached this low point? What had I done? Only a short time ago I had been a prosperous entrepreneur. I had started a company out of the back of the very same pickup truck I was now changing in, and the project had become so successful that my partner and I had more than a hundred employees working in a building that we owned, along with some land, and were netting more than 150 million dollars a year in profits. I had been the president, the leader, and I had passed through most airports in the world to create what was becoming our own little empire. But, as one learns through life's chapters, the mistakes we make and traps we set for ourselves tend to follow us like shadows. For me, the same old issues never faded away. In this case, I had committed a familiar sin: I had trusted too much. The company sank and split apart.

The legal morass was crippling, and not only emotionally. I had no income, and the bills—attorneys', mortgage, and so on— had piled up on me so fast I was worried about bankruptcy. What was I going to do for work? Where was I going to live? After a lifetime, I had finally built my own house in the High Sierra. It was constructed of wood milled from sixty thousand feet of timber sprawling over 120 acres, all of which I had been forced to sell to cover my growing expenses. Also on the chopping block was *Celebration,* my sixty-foot sailboat, which I and my captain (well, former captain; I had to let him go too) had returned to our winter berth in Miami, following the most fabulous passage through the Caribbean from Trinidad. I was never desirous of owning fancy cars: my '65 Ford pickup could go anywhere. The diesel behemoth would do, but with my dwindling finances I must confess the feelings of panic, anxiety, and dread were overbearing. How was I going to survive? Could I go back to show business after such a long absence?

I remembered those presentations in hotels, boardrooms, and church basements when I imagined myself to be onstage, trying to perfect my performance. Someday, I thought, I might get another chance. Now I had it: Once again, I had to start over.

At least that was something I had a lot of experience with.

But I wasn't eighteen or twenty-three anymore. I wasn't thirty-five or forty-five. I was in my late sixties, past the age of retirement, and looking to start fresh in a world and economy that was far faster than I was, and hyperdigital as well. Too many buttons to push. Too few people left to speak with. I had become an alien.

I was in survival mode, conserving every dollar. Instead of enjoying the comforts of a hotel room before an audition, ensuring that I got a good rest, I had crashed in the back of my pickup and was living like a hobo. Maybe I had become a hobo, I thought, now getting dressed outside my truck for the audition. I had a sport jacket that I wore on special occasions, folded in the back with a camping stove and other gear. Sitting on the open tailgate, I put on my pants, socks, and loafers and was reminded of my first days in Hollywood, hauling industrial waste around the city to earn a few extra dollars and changing into my suit in my garbage truck, which I used to get to auditions. More than forty years had passed! Had anything changed? Christ, I couldn't even play a lobster on ice skates in one stupid commercial.

I had no mirror to use. For some last-minute grooming, I leaned in front of the side mirror of my truck with my razor, trimming a few spots on my beard line without shaving cream or hot water, and in the reflection of my truck's mirror I was again confronted with myself, the immense challenge of trying to resurrect a career in front of me, my past gnawing at me, and the inescapable burden of that most precious commodity: time. It always hurtles along too fast, and no matter how hard you try to slow it down, you never have a chance to get any of it back. Had I spent my days wisely? Could I have done more?

I hopped into the truck, turned over the gears, and pulled out of the campground, a cloud of diesel smoke behind me. Out on a familiar road, all those memories came to me—of the nights we set campfires out by Point Dume; and that time I helped save a girl who was drowning in Malibu; and the other time the lifeguards had to come save me and Rosie, a red-haired, freckle-faced beauty I had coaxed into the water (and then out of her bathing suit) before we both got swept up in a riptide. Indeed, my finest moments had not cost a dime, financed instead by a mix of courage, boldness, and stupidity.

I thought back over the many years of auditions. Getting my energy up. Being on when I was really falling apart. How would I handle another disappointment at my age?

I pulled out the instructions that Barbara, my new agent, had given me for the audition.

The address was 200 South La Brea; the time, one o'clock. It was a casting facility, one of hundreds peppered throughout Hollywood, a place I hadn't been to in years. I knew very little about the gig, only a few scraps of information that Barbara had told me over the phone. It was a commercial role for a beer company. Heineken had a new campaign they wanted to launch for Dos Equis, a beer that needed a boost in their Latino market, and was hiring a new spokesman of sorts for the brand. What specifically were they looking for?

"They want a Hemingway kind of guy," she said. "That's you!"

I wasn't so sure. Dos Equis had a Latino market. I was not Latino.

"Honey, I'm all wrong for this," I told her.

"Just give it your best and then forget about it," she said.

I asked her for instructions. Was there any script to read? Any storyboard?

"They want improv," she said. "You can do any kind of monologue you want, but you have to end with their line."

"What's the line?" I asked her.

"No matter where you start your monologue, you have to end with the line 'And that's how I arm-wrestled Fidel Castro,'" she said.

The engine of the truck grinding beneath me, I pulled out onto the Pacific Coast Highway. I searched my past. A life of lessons, some learned the hard way, some learned laughing, some learned in the heat of passion or the cold of rejection. So many lessons—but had any given me a clue as to how I could have ever come to arm-wrestle Fidel Castro?

Don't Get Left Behind

I didn't run away the first time. Mother did. I was only six weeks old, just a newborn swaddled in cloth. The supermarket was just at the bottom of the hill, only a few blocks from our apartment in Riverdale. I'll never know what happened next. I do know that Mother left the store, taking her groceries home, but she left one package behind.

Mind you, she was busy. And adored. She had started working for Conover's Cover Girls, a leading model agency run by Harry Conover, then the fashion czar of New York. The job was the gateway to fame, stardom, and fortune. She modeled sable pelts, feather boas, silk brassieres, hats, bathing suits. She was close friends with Lauren Bacall, who also started her career as one of Harry Conover's Cover Girls, and always ran late to auditions. Maybe that was why, in the bustle of juggling grocery parcels and a budding career, something had to get overlooked and left behind in the aisle of a supermarket.

9

Unfortunately, that something was an infant. And, most unfortunately, that infant was me.

When I asked her about it years later, at least her answer was honest.

"I just forgot," she said. But I never did.

It would not be the last time she left me someplace. When I was five years old, perhaps the earliest age a parent can legally send a child away, I was enrolled in Mrs. Hunt's Boarding School, a depository for errant children, in Cedarhurst, Long Island. My memories? Pulling up to the brick building in a taxi, dressed in a suit and tie, the late spring snow dusting over the windshield in flakes that quickly disappeared.

Mrs. Hunt was the headmistress, and she scared me. Even at that age I could recognize an attractive woman, but her blue eyes were cold, austere, and judgmental. My mother and I sat across from her at her desk, my legs dangling from the seat. Mrs. Hunt listened as Mother told her how I had become a difficult child at home.

The problem was, I was listening too. Apparently, I was a naughty, unloving, unmanageable boy. This was news to me. I wanted to speak up. She's lying! But, being five, I was not adept at personal representation. So I just sat there, and soon I was watching the taillights of her taxi disappear through the windows. I chased after her, and when I knew she was not coming back and I could not catch her, I hid under the yellow flowers of a forsythia bush, already in bloom in spite of the late snowfall. As I had yet to learn the finer intricacies of covert operations, I was soon discovered, picked up under the arms by Mrs. Hunt, and ferried through the dorm, which for some reason smelled like burned toast, and into a quaint room. I watched the heavy door close behind me.

The truth was, I wasn't a bad kid. I just missed my father. And imagining him coming to rescue me, wearing the maroon Woolrich coat he always did when we went fishing, the hood hanging back over his shoulders, got me through my days. When was he coming to get me?

At night, I cried myself to sleep at Mrs. Hunt's, staring at the ceiling. My mother was wrong about me, and I knew it. If I had known more about her past or had the ability to understand that she was doing her best, it would have been different. But I was a five-year-old; my emotional maturity and deep sense of empathy were less than developed.

Your Body Can Do Anything You Put Your Mind To

The truth is, Mother was not suited for parenthood, a predilection that was not her fault. Her own mother had died in front of her, suffering a stroke in a shop the family ran in Brooklyn. Her untimely death left my mother, Greta, and her older brother, Eli, to fend for themselves. They had their father, my grandfather Alexander, but he was a radical eccentric, an intellectual, and a drifter. And after my grandmother's death, drift he did.

Alexander was disabled, so it's amazing he drifted so far, landing on that pirate boat off Costa Rica and living for a time on a Navajo reservation. As a young child he developed a bone disease, osteomyelitis, and his legs never grew. His disease was difficult to treat professionally. So he treated it himself, most unprofessionally: On his shin, there was deep open wound that revealed his faulty bones. He'd take out his pocketknife, flip open the blade, and start carving away at his shin bone, eliciting a terrible odor that reminded me of rotten meat. I don't know why cutting up his own leg caused such a foul smell or why it was therapeutic, but I do know it happened. I assure you. I saw it.

As odd as he was, Alexander was an inspiration. To compensate for his failing legs, he followed an intense muscle-building regimen for his upper torso, which came to resemble that of a Greek god. He was so strong he could perform an iron cross, a gymnast's maneuver in which he suspended himself between two steel rings with his arms held horizontally. And yet he couldn't even walk on his own. To steady himself, my grandfather used a shillelagh, a cane made from dark hardwood, which doubled as a cudgel to threaten anyone who disagreed with his Bolshevik politics, which was just about everyone.

He was hardly a nurturing soul. Once, I remember Flight, our springer spaniel, jumped up on the nightstand and ate my grandfather's dentures, then washed them down with a delicious black slipper. Grandpa was pissed. Shillelagh in one hand raised for battle and the surviving slipper in the other, he hobbled spastically after the frightened dog, frantically whipping the air with the footwear.

"I'll kill that fucking mutt," he said, expectorating brown spittle from the Ivanhoe tobacco curled up in his lip. In his frenetic effort to attack the dog, he lost his balance. But the poor dog lost much more. Terrified, Flight sprinted toward the second-floor window and, true to his name, jumped out. (The dog survived his fall, but he ended up with a limp, just like Grandpa.)

Grandpa was caustic and unpredictable, but he was a dreamer, and his mind swirled with energy and fantastic ideas. He was an amateur mason and liked working with stone, and one of his many cockeyed ideas was to invent a doghouse made from concrete. If he could prefab the design (God knows how), he calculated a massive fortune would follow. Not surprisingly, the cement doghouse never made it to market, but his own personal adventure stories were so riveting, they would inspire my own wayward travels. I remember him describing the way he converted his Model A Ford into a camper, retrofitting the back into his own sleeping quarters in which he caravaned across the country. I can almost see him stopping at those Navajo reservations, regaling the Native American chiefs there with tales of his travels and teaching them herbal remedies found in nature, or, more likely, the Yiddish theater. During the Great Depression he'd arrived in Los Angeles and, with his knowledge about the body and his own natural strength, helped found Muscle Beach. Then he was off to Central America. I never learned how he found work as a cook on a pirate ship, but he did tell me they smuggled mahogany out of Costa Rica. His was a wild life, but as he explored the world, Mother and Eli were left at home to fend for each other.

There Are All Different Kinds
of Heroes

Before he disappeared to trek around the world in search of adventure, Alexander left the custody of my mother and her brother, Eli, to a handful of relatives, who shuffled them between their homes like playing cards. The pride of the family was Eli, who first lived in Jackson Heights with Uncle Louis. Uncle Louis worked part-time as a masseuse in the Catskill resorts, never went anywhere without a cigar in his mouth, shot craps in his basement, and possessed the family gene that made him sharply critical of everyone except himself. A cast of cantankerous characters—Cousin Paul, Uncle Max, Cousin Herbie, and Monroe, each a bit eccentric in his own special way—also helped raise my mother and Eli for a while. Not having a family or place of their own left its mark. Eli and my mother rarely had their own clothes as children, always the recipients of hand-me-downs from the cousins and other family members. My mother dreamed of a better life—or at least clothes that were her own—for herself and Eli.

Soon, she would dream only for herself.

My uncle Eli graduated from the Naval Academy in Annapolis, and, since the war had begun, he was promptly shipped out to one of the farthest outposts: the South Pacific theater.

With her mother gone and her absentee father wandering the country in his camper, my mother's closest family member was Eli. He raised her as best he could. Back in New York, along with her relatives, she eagerly read his letters from the front. Shortly after the letters stopped, the military car arrived with the navy's regrets from Washington. There had been an attack. He had been on a destroyer, working as a lieutenant. It was a dangerous assignment, considering Japanese destroyers owned those waters. Inevitably, a kamikaze pilot had attacked them.

Inside their boat, the sailors were rocked, scrambling to put out fires and keep the oncoming water from sinking the ship. Eli was down in the hull, pushing through the chambers, trying to close the large doors to keep more water from coming onboard. The water kept rising, though. He came to a door and started to close it, but there was no way to close it and get to safety behind it. As the water filled up the chamber around him, he grabbed the wheel and started turning it to lock the door tight, ensuring that the others might have a chance to live and guaranteeing that he would not.

Many years later, long after the war, Mother traveled to the South Pacific to visit the grave marker with his name on it, which had been placed in New Caledonia. She must have wondered why the forces of nature had colluded so heavily against her, first making her father disabled, then taking her mother before her own eyes, and finally leaving her hero brother dead in foreign waters. Without Eli, my mother's only protector was gone.

It's one thing to understand the magnitude of these losses, one after another, intellectually. It's quite another to understand them emotionally. It took me some years to comprehend it all. About fifty, if we're being honest. But, many, many years later, on a dock overlooking a lake in Arizona, my mother and I would talk, deeply, honestly, sincerely. She would apologize. And I would forgive her. I came to understand that her circumstances cornered her and drove her to selfishness. With everyone gone, she'd had to fend for herself, she must have thought. And maybe that's why she occasionally left me. And why she left my father.

He was a jock and a bon vivant of his own making. Sure, he had dreams of fortune, but my dad, Milton, was always more than satisfied with what was in front of him. He had been a semipro basketball player for a brief time, standing at the towering height of five foot eight, and was so quick on his feet that he beat the New York City quarter-mile champ in a race once, wearing street shoes. He trained boxers and became a physical education teacher, an outdoorsman, and a fly-fishing fanatic. He had the bank account to show for it.

When I was a boy, my uncle Herbie, my dad's brother, once told me, "Your father is the most successful man I know."

"Why?" I asked.

"Because he has no ambition at all."

His love was always good enough for me. Mother always wanted more. A quick divorce was imminent, and after she married my wealthy stepfather and carted me off to the suburbs, I was always trying to find my way back to my father. I'd escape during the middle of the day and at night. I'd sneak onto trains, run from the Harlem stop to his apartment, and listen to him in the other room on the phone with my mother.

"I've got him," he'd say, and in the days or hours we could spend together, I'd have him, following him everywhere. He was my protector, my hero.

"Someday you'll understand," he'd said about the fight and ensuing legal battle over my custody. He was right. Eventually, I understood. But eventually takes a long time to arrive.

You Are Who You Know

In the mornings, I'd stay on the couch under the sheets he kept for me in the closet and listen to him leave about half an hour before the sun came up. He'd kiss me on the forehead, then disappear out the front door to do roadwork. For a time, he was managing a prizefighter, an Irish prospect turned stumblebum named Jerry McCarthy, whose idea of roadwork was six miles followed by at least six Tom Collinses.

"He's a coward," he told me about McCarthy. "He can only fight when he's drunk."

After those runs, he'd dress up, slipping his coach's whistle around his neck, and wait for the Colonel. The Colonel was an odd character who, like so many, adored my father; in his case, so much so that he volunteered to be his chauffeur. The Colonel was the owner of an old Lincoln that was so beat-up it would have drawn glares and jeers in Tijuana. My father didn't care what the car looked like. He saluted him with ceremony every morning.

"Colonel, take me uptown," he'd say, snapping his hand in a salute like a field commander.

"Yes, sir," the Colonel would say, saluting with the wrong hand and steering his limousine of sorts in the direction of James Monroe, the high school where my father worked, in Fort Apache, then and now one of the most dangerous neighborhoods in the Bronx. There he maintained an eclectic group of friends—the maintenance staff, the crossing guards—and during breaks he would disappear into the boiler room to take a slug from his discreetly stashed bottle of Hiram Walker bourbon and play a few games of pinochle with the janitors and other coaches. He never spent the money he earned in those card games on himself; instead, he used his winnings on new uniforms, shoes, and equipment for students who couldn't afford them. He must have been up in winnings one year, because he financed his own basketball team and snuck them into the high school league.

So my uncle was wrong. My father had one ambition: basketball.

Fort Tyron Prep, he called his team, a joke considering how poor the students—a term I'm using liberally—were. Those kids couldn't have afforded a free tour of prep school, let alone prep school. They came from Harlem and the Bronx, when they came to school at all. But he mentored them so closely they became a championship team. He snuck them into the city's interschool league, where they defeated many of the New York City teams. Eventually, they were bused up to West Point to take on the junior varsity program there. Soon, the reporters who covered high school sports—even from *The New York Times*—picked up the story. My father worked so hard for those kids. He even helped more than a few of them earn scholarships, including three brothers, who, despite their impoverished upbringing, all attended and graduated from Yale.

For a team photo, my father took them all to Columbia University, and they posed in front of the Ivy League walls themselves. The photo would be a treasure for them. And for him.

He never left me at home when I visited, never left me out of anything. I was in the locker room. I was out in the fields with him coaching the cross-country team in Van Cortlandt Park. I followed him to Yankee Stadium or to the Meadowlands—even to the local athletic clubs, the Y, and the armories—for weeknight boxing smokers.

"Colonel, take me to the Garden," he'd say, and outside the arena, amid the mobs, he'd greet his friends on the way into the venue. We sat on the bench of the New York Knickerbockers as Red Holzman, one of his friends, coached the team and when Goose Tatum and Meadowlark Lemon of the Harlem Globetrotters came through. After games, I'd follow him to mill in front of the players' locker rooms or near the entrance, where he greeted coaches and other friends.

"Hey, Bob," he'd say, introducing me to Bob Mathias, the famous decathlon champion.

"Hey, Jerry," he'd say, introducing me to Jerry McGarity, the renowned high school swimming coach and a strange, hard-drinking Irishman. (McGarity had a friend who worked at Sing Sing, and it always bothered my father that he took perverse pleasure in watching the executions there.) One summer night, my father crossed the street and stopped. "Hey, Jim," he said, introducing me to Jim Thorpe, the famous Native American Olympian who earned his medals without a pair of shoes and was now a homeless drunk, sleeping in the gutter.

He even introduced me to the Great Zbyszko, the famous wrestler, who was close to my father. During the Depression, the contests between the world's strongest men, wrestlers, and grapplers were popular, and my father marveled at their training regimens. The Great Zbyszko had come from Poland via Vienna, was a heady intellectual, and taught my father the secrets for accumulating massive strength. Zbyszko was so strong he could take a handful of bottle caps, place them between his fingers, and squeeze them all together. He could also tear a New York City phone book in half. Years later he told my father the secret to the trick. Didn't matter. I was impressed.

Together, my father and the Great Zbyszko hatched a scheme during the Depression to make their own bathtub gin. Zbyszko showed my father how to do it, rolling out the vapors in a towel, which was the secret to their high-quality product.

My father's closest friends, though, were not the famous athletes but the unknown masters of their craft, the hands behind the stars, the great cornermen and cut men and the network of self-appointed doctors, healers, seconds, and spit-bucket shamans.

E very day with my father was an adventure. We often stopped off at the Abercrombie & Fitch store on Fifth Avenue, where he purchased his feathers and other supplies to tie his flies for fishing. I loved these trips to Abercrombie, and veering inside the gun room and marveling at these incredible wild animals that had been shot and stuffed, I imagined myself a hunter too, venturing out into the bush with my gun bearers to face these marvelous beasts. The danger was riveting, putting oneself out in front of a charging rhino or water buffalo, a species considered the most dangerous game in the world. As a gift, my father gave me my first gun: a pump-action Winchester .22. I could shoot only when my father took me to the range or into the woods, but I loved shooting with him and was a good marksman. Years later, I was part of a team that won the national summer camp competition. It was small-bore, twenty-two-caliber class, fifty feet. I shot 97/100, not perfect, but still incredibly accurate.

When I wasn't with my father, I'd substitute adventure books for adventure. I devoured stories that would place me high in the Andes of Peru or the Himalayas of Tibet or amid the tall grass on the plains of the Serengeti. I was in awe of the African interior.

At night, before going to bed, my father passed me his T-shirt to sleep in, the faded gray cotton reaching down over my knees. I've had trouble sleeping all my life, but never in that shirt. It was like a shield, and my father was my protector.

Cultivate Eccentric Influences

Sunday at Uncle Mike's was an education in itself. Unlike my mother's side of the family, which perhaps never got over the tragedies of losing my grandmother to her illness and my uncle Eli, who never came home from the war, my father's people were exuberant, eccentric, and dedicated to scouring the world in search of adventure. I remember my father introducing me to his cousins, who mesmerized me with their tales. Uncle Mike, for instance, was the proprietor of Agnes Strong Imports, a downtown curiosity shop that rivaled city museums. I peered through the bows and arrows, rugs, chandeliers, and other oddities from his world travels, and he gave me a chess set made from real ivory, no doubt a souvenir he'd picked up on his travels across the Serengeti. He later developed a friendship with Pancho Villa and traveled extensively throughout Mexico. As a teenager, he had found his way into a senior job building the railroad in Brazil and ultimately lived for a time with the Yaqui Indians. They taught him the finer points of marksmanship.

"Jono," Uncle Mike would say, using my nickname, "the Yaqui can shoot from horseback and hit their target on a moving train, always in the same place: right between the eyes!"

Uncle John, Uncle Mike's brother, was not a spy, but he worked in the Office of Strategic Services, or the OSS, the precursor to the CIA. He was a scrapper, tough and strong, and relished a good fight. My father used to say, "Whenever we heard sirens, we always worried about Johnny."

After the war, Uncle John became a druggist and worked in a pharmacy. He was so tough that, once, when an armed gunman pointed a pistol at his head, demanding the cash in the drawer, Uncle John disarmed him single-handedly and called the police to pick up the poor bastard. At the time, Uncle John was eighty-three.

Uncle Abe, another brother, had a small bootlegging operation in Milwaukee. Always the practical man, Abe delivered his bootleg hooch from a street trolley car, where he served as the conductor, hiding the bottles behind the driver's seat on his routes.

"Hold!" he'd call out to the passengers, then scamper off to make his deliveries. Uncle Abe fancied himself an astute businessman, buying, for instance, a tomato farm on a street called Worth Avenue, in then the sleepy Florida farm town of West Palm Beach. In a few years, he sold the tomato farm for a few thousand in profit, thinking he'd become a mogul after closing the biggest deal of his lifetime. Now that land is among the most expensive stretches of real estate in the world.

ACT I

His sister, Henrietta Strong, another accomplished immigrant, helped found a home for poor children in Greenwich Village. She also started a greeting card company called Brownie Block Prints, which she eventually sold to Hallmark for millions. For her efforts, she was awarded Woman of the Year by Eleanor Roosevelt.

And let's not forget Uncle Ezra, touched by madness, a poet given to melancholy, a raconteur and lothario of note, who made the bohemian coffee shops of Greenwich Village his home and suffered an untimely demise at his own hand. Or Uncle Julius, the romantic hobo and wanderer who would arrive unannounced at the farm of Aunt Jenny, the mother of Mike, Ezra, John, and Abe, make a few repairs to the tractors and threshers, then disappear at sunset to scratch the wanderlust itch that consumed him all his life.

When I was a young man, these eccentrics were my teachers, my living encyclopedia of adventure, and I learned about the world through their exploits. My father learned from them too. He and his cousins were the new generation, desperate to explore America and the world once Isadore and Minnie, his parents, settled in New York after emigrating from Riga, Latvia. His father arrived with a fifty-dollar gold piece and dreams of a new life, leaving behind a bleak existence and little hope for prosperity. But like many others, they found a way.

Know Your Roots

Isadore Goldsmith, my grandfather, was a model of kindness. After passing through Ellis Island and settling in the Bronx, he opened a candy and cigar store near Yankee Stadium, then a focal point in the nation, considering the batting records Babe Ruth was setting.

Ruth was one of my grandfather's most loyal customers. My grandfather could always tell when the Babe was coming because he could hear the gales of laughter from a crush of children that always surrounded the slugger, following him from every direction.

Ruth was an avid cigar smoker, and he'd lift a glass jar in my grandfather's store, reach in with his giant paw, and retrieve a handful of stogies each day.

"Izzy, put it on the bill," he'd say, and wander off, a chubby Pied Piper with the children trailing after him.

My grandfather would wake up before dawn, take a shot of

slivovitz with his coffee, then wait for an Irish cop to meet him and accompany him to fetch his bundle of newspapers and escort him to his store, because the neighborhood was so dangerous. Particularly in the dark of early morning.

"Let's go, Izzy," the cop would say in his Irish brogue, knocking at the door, and my grandfather would lace up his black high-button shoes and disappear into the darkness of the morning and the hostile streets.

Isadore was gentle and honest, yet he tried to be proper and formal in every facet of his life. To all his suppliers and vendors, for instance, he signed his paperwork with the same closing: "And obliged, I. Goldsmith." He was proud of that, and he toiled for years, never taking a break. Finally, the family decided to send him on a vacation. To New Jersey. He didn't want to go. He'd never been on a vacation, and he certainly didn't want to start in his advanced years. All he knew was work. But they sent him away anyway, despite his protests. A few days later, my grandmother received the following note from him:

> My Dear Minnie,
> I want to come home. I'm going crazy. I can't sleep.
> There's no noise. It's too quiet. Can I come home? I love
> you. I miss you, Herbie, and Milton.
> And Obliged, I. Goldsmith

What a salutation. He may have only sold candy and cigars, but he did so with pride and humility. I can still see his weathered hands and remember the fun we had playing the "hand game"—the one where one player places his or her hands over the other person's hands, and the bottom player tries to slap the upper hands before they are pulled away. I never knew the name of the game. But I didn't need to know specifics to have fun playing it with Grandpa. He smelled like old newspapers, and that was a good thing.

My grandma stood all of four foot ten, but she stood tall. A spirited woman, a woman to be reckoned with, she was a suffragist who marched down Fifth Avenue with William Gompes (the head of the Shirtwaist Union), and made the best blintzes I ever tasted. She ran the roost and later was president of the Over 80 Club at the shul.

Adventure Is What
You Make of It

Brant Lake was a summer camp in the Adirondacks, just down the road from the Borscht Belt, where the scions of the *schmatte* (also known as the garment industry) sent their children to summer camp. With his gentle demeanor, experience in sports, and off-season job as a teacher in physical education, my father was a natural choice to be head counselor and run activities during the summer. He couldn't afford the fee to send me. So he made sure I was part of the deal with the camp's owners to secure him.

I can still see Brant Lake Camp itself, a collection of wooden cabins nestled under the long arms of trees, the forest covered in pine needles, and bunks that smelled of musk and pine sap. The center of the camp was the lake itself, an oasis of freshwater where I learned to swim and dive. I remember my father holding out his hands to catch me. I would jump to him, overflowing with joy. I trusted him completely.

This was during the war years. At night there was the crackling of radios that some of the counselors, as well as the older kids in the bunk, huddled around to listen to reports of the Germans bombing Paris and live broadcasts of Joe Louis making his campaign through the heavyweight division. During the day, we played the usual camp games, like color war, set off in our canoes, and learned how to shoot with bows and arrows. If I was lucky, my father would have an hour to spare, and we'd set out to the edge of the lake with our rods to make a few casts in a spot where he thought I'd have a good chance to catch a fish, if only I could keep the hook out of the trees and not tangled on my pants or stuck in his fingers.

When the time wasn't right to fish, we'd go on adventures. I remember him taking me on a hike through the woods after camp one afternoon.

"We need to be careful," he said cautiously, looking around.

"Why's that?" I asked.

"This is Indian country," he murmured, slowing down, careful not to make sounds with the forest floor crunching underfoot. I slowed down too, peering through the trees, expecting to see a flash of feathers from a headdress, a smear of war paint, or a charging horse coming our way.

Then, up the path, my father pointed at a tree.

"Look," he said, concerned, and as I followed the line of sight leading from his finger, I saw it. It was an arrow, wedged in the tree.

I moved closer to him.

"Let's go back," I said. "Let's go look for Indians another time."

"And look over there," he said, getting excited. There was another arrow in another tree.

I grasped his hand tightly, fearful of an imminent attack.

"Don't worry, son," he said, patting my head reassuringly. "We can handle them."

When he was there, I knew we could.

I was in awe of him, and so were the others in the camp, for his quiet control and masterful handling of conflicts. All the kids looked up to him. But they couldn't have him. He was *my* father.

Only years later did I realize my father had placed those arrows in the trees. Incidentally, this would not be my last experience with bows and arrows at camp. But that's a story that will come much, much later.

The Longer It Waits,
the More the Truth Hurts

I remember one time in particular when I lied to him. He taught me something I would never forget. We were at Brant Lake, and I was in the dining room with my bunkmates. The dining room was in a larger building, like a log cabin with long wooden tables. We all were sitting down when another boy approached our table with his food tray.

I was always on the lookout for ways to get a laugh, so I stood up, pretending to be a gentleman, and pulled out a chair for my bunkmate. Just as he was about to sit down, I yanked away the chair. The boy fell instantly, crashing onto the dining room floor, in pain, his dinner splattered all over his shirt and pants and the floorboards of the mess hall. All the others at the table were howling with laughter. I'd done my job, entertaining them to get their approval. Mission accomplished. I got a cheap laugh at my buddy's expense.

"What happened?" one counselor said, rushing over and looking at the fallen boy and his lost dinner.

I was grinning.

"You did that?" the counselor said.

"No," I said. "It was an accident."

The counselor didn't buy it.

"I want you to go to your father, and I want you to tell him what you did," he said.

As head counselor, my father sat with the older campers. It was the longest walk of my life, heading over to his table in shame. My chin was quivering in fear, as I wondered what he'd do. I'd never had to confront him like this.

"Daddy, I didn't do anything," I said. "I got into trouble for something that I didn't do."

He didn't yell at me. He patted me on the shoulder, calming me down. I survived! And I was confused. Could lying be this simple?

Later that night, I was about to fall asleep when my father entered the bunk and took his seat on the edge of my cot as he usually did. He didn't start with his usual bedtime story.

"Son, I think that you didn't tell me the truth today," he said.

I sunk into my cot, wishing I could hide. I couldn't tell if the other boys were listening to our conversation, but I lowered my voice to keep them from hearing.

"I lied to you, Daddy," I said in a petrified whisper.

For a moment, he didn't say anything. Then he put his arm around me.

"Well, if you lie to me, I blame myself," he said. "There must be something about me that you can't tell me the truth. And I feel very badly about that."

Wait a second. Why would he blame himself for a prank that I pulled?

The guilt was overwhelming. My father had done nothing wrong. I was the culprit. I didn't have the courage to tell the truth. As he turned the tables, I learned a very important lesson. I never lied to him again.

That's not exactly true.

I never lied to him again, except for one other time. There are a lot of stories I'll tell. That won't be one of them. It is mine, and mine alone, to live with.

Your Most Prized Possessions Shouldn't Be Possessions

My father loved to fly-fish. He also loved the gear, the philosophy, and the craftsmanship that he could put into it. He grew up in New York City, so how he learned to fish I'll never know, nor did I ever learn the origin of his passion for the sport. Some kids have dads who teach them golf. Others play baseball or soccer. We fished. We'd spend the weekends waking up at dawn to head upstate to fish the Esopus, the Neversink, and the Beaverkill or just to tune up his equipment. He tied beautiful flies. He sent away for the finest equipment from around the world: His hooks came from England, as did the oilskin pouch he used for tobacco. There were reels from Hardy, a famous manufacturer, that were the best to use—and the most expensive. He used a tiny sharpener to hone his hooks, and he picked up fly feathers from Abercrombie—peacock furl and wings, necks of pheasant, and gamecock plumage. When he caught the first fish of the day, he'd place his tackle box, complete with a little vise attached to hold the hook, on a rock. He'd open up the belly of the fish with his knife to see what the fish were eating, then implement a process that's called "matching the hatch," or tying a fly to mimic the fishes' diet.

It was an art form, and he loved his equipment so much. Yet he gave me complete, unfettered access to it. Sometimes, I couldn't understand why. One time we were on Lake Mahopac in upper Westchester County, New York. My mind was elsewhere. I had been fighting with my mother and stepfather. Staring out into the ether, wondering how I could escape them and live with my father, I dropped his favorite Hardy reel.

I reached to grab it, but I was too late. In the water, I watched the reel slowly shine and flip and flop and shine until it could be seen no more, gone into the murky depths. I panicked. I'd lost one of my father's most treasured possessions. I worried he would be very upset—and more so if he knew what I'd been thinking about when it happened. But instead he put his arm around me and told me not to worry.

"It's only a reel," he said. He went to the car, came back with a spare. "Let's keep fishing."

He never made me feel guilty for anything. Not that he always approved of my choices. He was firm but fair and loving. He loved the finer things for their utility. To him, objects weren't to be enshrined and worshipped.

"If it's any good, don't leave it hanging on a wall," he'd say.

Every Challenge Is a Chance to Build Your Strength

Eventually, visitation time would end. I'd get back into my father's car, and he'd drive me to the Scarsdale train station, where my mother would be waiting impatiently to pick me up. My mother loathed anything to do with my father. Anything he gave me and I liked, she looked to take away. My cherished BB gun and literary portals to sub-Saharan Africa would be first, I knew, after I'd gotten endless chores and instructions I am sure had been specifically tailored to upset me. Perhaps they were going to force me to change my ways and finally become a good boy. Not likely.

If I was hungry, she restricted the food. Or forced me to eat things I didn't like. As a child, I had a poor reaction to eating fish. So fish made its way onto the menu frequently, along with the dreaded spinach and the other vegetables I liked least. I loathed the color brown; sure enough, the outfits she picked for me ranged the spectrum from brown to other shades of brown. I was routinely sentenced to hard labor in the backyard, forced to endure hours in the summer heat obeying her dictatorial orders and trying to keep pace with her constantly changing mind: these flowers here, those bushes there. My playtime was directly related to my work output: no swimming until the work was done. Conveniently for her, the work was never done. I can still hear her screaming at me, preparing me for a life as a serf.

One day, I excitedly ran home from school to show her the first B I ever got. I was so proud. "Fine," she remarked. "But it should have been an A." My incredible achievement in scholarship, dashed.

The best part about home was the drive to and from home with my father. There was a wonderful feeling when his 1947 Mercury would arrive at the railroad station on visiting day. The car sported cracked paint, broken-in seats, and a large trunk that doubled as a gym locker—stuffed with fishing reels and rods, tackle boxes, basketballs, baseball bats, old gym shoes and towels, a jump rope, a deck of playing cards, and a few sets of dice. But it was his chariot. In that car he spirited me away. In that car he taught me to drive. I was eight. He was a jock, and while he was always dreaming up an invention or two, a scheme that could have made him and his good-time friends who lingered around Madison Square Garden rich, he liked nothing more than healthy competition. He adored the time with his friends, his fishing, and me.

When the visits ended, always too soon, my mother would stand there waiting, the engine of her car running, pressuring me to hurry up. I tried not to cry. I wasn't always successful. Sometimes, my father wasn't either.

"Flex your muscles, kid," he'd say, pointing to my puny biceps. "Life is a long game. We're only at the beginning."

What's in a Name
Matters Less Than What's in
the One Who's Named

Unlike my father, Jerome S. Lippe was the embodiment of wealth. My stepfather had manicured nails coated in that matte polish you're not supposed to notice but always do. His hair was combed so perfectly that not one stray hair got away from the others. He wore things I had never even seen before: shiny cuff links, silk Sulka ties only, silk handkerchiefs, and imported watches, the entire ensemble monogrammed with "JSL," his initials. He also wore high socks with sock garters, ensuring that a wrinkle would never form under his trouser leg. He smelled of Vetiver and Vitalis and was always draped in a custom suit and reeked of arrogance and pomposity.

Jerome was a successful manufacturer of housewares. He had his own company, Leipzig and Lippe, and an interest in a company called Basketville, out of Putney, Vermont, that made baskets of all varieties. He also manufactured barbecue grills, which he claimed to have invented. Apparently, he had never heard of cavemen. He met my mother through another model working in his showroom and proceeded to buy her. Just like other things he wanted. She never put up too much resistance. He first asked her to model for him. She had always wanted to be an interior designer, and he offered her a position in his company. She was talented and ambitious. She went about redesigning his baskets, offering a unique touch: hand-painting them. His business grew greatly as a result, and they spent a lot of time together. My father's suspicions were inevitable and soon after proved true. A divorce was imminent.

After their wedding in Havana, Cuba, we all moved in together at 10 Park Avenue, a luxury hotel in Manhattan, and Jerome began to shower me with a number of wonderful bribes in exchange for my affection. I happily played my first role. I remember the giant yellow balloon he'd given me for my birthday, along with an armada of toys and a personal introduction to his world. His office was on Broadway and Twenty-Sixth Street, only a few blocks from the hotel where we lived, and I'd accompany him during the workday when not in school. Every morning we'd have the same breakfast—scrambled eggs, moist; white toast, buttered heavily; bacon, crisp; orange juice—all presented to us by his servants, from a collection of silver pieces, like we were royalty. We'd head into the office and receive many warm salutes from his employees, whose affection had been purchased, like that of everyone else he came into contact with. I'd follow him to the barbershop after work, where we were greeted by Maurice, his barber, who quickly made his face disappear in a combination of hot towels and mounds of shaving cream. Then it was on to the Old Crow Restaurant, where he kept his own table.

"This is my son," he'd say proudly, showing me off to the maître d' and waitstaff. I always smiled and played along, but deep inside, I knew I wasn't his son. And he wasn't my father.

The honeymoon was over quickly. Living in a hotel was claustrophobic, and we soon moved out to Scarsdale, a ritzy enclave in Westchester County, outside the city. The house itself was not as large as a mansion, but it was close, and Mother had all the accoutrements she wanted, plus her garden and gardeners. And the unpaid staff: me.

She decorated each room, picked the wallpaper, and soon began quarreling with Jerome over a variety of issues—again, involving me. Jerome, a smug and arrogant man, could not accept the fact that I would never treat him like a father, and once it became clear that he could not buy my affection and we'd never get along, he turned on me, assigning me chores and tasks "to teach me a lesson." I've remained unclear all my life what the moral value of fetching him scotch and freshening up the jar of peanuts during the Giants football game truly was. He wanted a son of his own, but after birthing me and being saddled with all the burdens of motherhood, Mother did not want to have another child.

That's probably why he coerced me into giving up my father's name. It would be easier to use Lippe, he told me, as it was constantly uncomfortable having to explain my different name in school. It tore me apart to abandon my father's name, but characteristically, my father put up little resistance. He said he allowed it to happen because he hoped it would make things easier for me.

Shakespeare once wrote, "What's in a name?" For me, every-thing. It wasn't until 1975 that I reclaimed my birthright. Shortly after I did, I was making a collect call and was asked to spell it out.

"G-O-L-D-S-M-I-T-H," I declared into the phone.

"You sound like you like your name," the operator said.

She had no idea.

Changing my name to Lippe didn't make any difference any-way. My mother and stepfather bickered endlessly, blaming me for the problem of the day. I, in turn, blamed them. And it became clear to all parties involved: I had to escape suburbia for good.

Sometimes, You Gotta Believe in Magic

My plan was to run away and never come back. For help, I had a coconspirator, One-Eyed Betty, our housekeeper.

"You best believe those motherfuckers had the voodoo; they had the curse," Betty Sharpe would tell me, pouring me a finger of scotch from my parents' liquor cabinet and teaching me about Haitian spells. She was born in Haiti, and I can still see her in her rolled-up stockings, puffy feet hiding in the men's high-top basketball sneakers she wore. I called her One-Eyed Betty because her left eye was cockeyed. Not to her face, of course. After all, she had the voodoo just as much as those motherfuckers she talked about did.

"Yeah, some of them motherfuckers are empowered," she'd say, talking about voodoo spells she knew about and their unlikely victims. "That baby turned around three times, one drop of blood fell from his nose, and he fell down to the earth dead."

I was barely old enough to leave the neighborhood, but Betty always treated me like an adult. On her day off, Betty went to Harlem to run the numbers, a street version of the lotto. But much of her adult life had been spent working for my stepfather and looking after his home. In the house, Betty became my confidante, and I became hers.

"Now, you know Maurice is fucking her. You know that," she'd say, referring to my friend's sexy mother and Maurice, a former shortstop for the Sing Sing baseball team. Fresh out of prison on parole, Maurice was working as Mrs. Schwartzbaum's handyman and, according to Betty, working on Mrs. Schwartzbaum as well. Betty was like a one-woman news bureau, absorbing every morsel of information in the house, overhearing phone calls, answering the front door, talking with the neighbors. She may have had only one good eye, but she saw all.

With my mother lost in her own tirades, Betty appointed herself my personal life coach. She always warned me to stay clear of promiscuous women.

"You just be careful with that little thing you've got right there," she'd say, warning me about venereal diseases. "That little thing you've got can give you some grief."

Boy, was she ever right.

With her knowledge of voodoo spells and wisdom, Betty was a lifesaver. She could also stand in for my father as my fishing companion when we'd head out to Croton Reservoir. She would unchain the wooden rowboat Mr. Lippe bought for me—maybe he wasn't all bad—and push it out on the water. I can picture her fat fingers and cracked hands on the oars and feel the water under the bow as she rowed us into the deeper part of the lake. Here, the sun warming my face, I could drop my line with a night crawler and wait for a perch or bass. She'd sit at the bow of the rowboat in her big-mammy straw hat, telling me stories about her encounters handling large venomous snakes and vicious mud-covered alligators in the Louisiana swamps.

We'd spend hours in the boat, waiting for a tug on the line.

"Motherfuckers ain't biting today," she'd say, gazing into the water and telling more of her stories about suburban adultery, the secrets of Haitian shamans, and seeing God.

I also designed my own safaris in Westchester County, taking along One-Eyed Betty as my personal gun bearer. We'd find a patch of woods and she'd follow me in.

"Stay back, I'll handle things," I told her seriously, marching into a patch of woods near Saks or Lord & Taylor, leading the way with my BB gun. So close to New York City, we couldn't hunt for gnu, gazelles, or water buffalo. So I had to settle for the most common big-game species indigenous to those parts: squirrel.

Betty proved a handy partner. Once, I hit a squirrel with a BB pellet and dropped him dead. Like a retriever, Betty waddled over, picked him up, removed the sheath knife she kept under her skirt, and proceeded to skin him. She then collected the necessary kindling and dead branches and made a campfire. In the glow of the flames I watched her fashion a spit from sticks, skewer the squirrel, and then bless him with a wailing voodoo prayer, hopping around the edge of the fire she'd built. As we feasted on barbecued squirrel, I asked Betty about that prayer and her fire dance.

"Hush up," she told me. "That's private."

Back in the house, Betty did her best to protect me. When

Mother would go on a tirade and lay into me, Betty stepped up and went to bat.

"Leave that boy alone," she'd tell my mother. But even Betty and her wisdom, kindness, and knowledge of voodoo could not alter my mother's chilly temperament.

"That woman is crazy," she'd tell me, throwing up her hands, returning to her chores, and leaving me to fend for myself. In my room, the door locked, I began to practice my own voodoo. I fashioned a mannequin and adorned it with female garments as a stand-in for my mother. I then brandished a machete I had stolen from the trunk of my father's car and danced around my bedroom, wailing the same voodoo prayer that Betty had around our roasted squirrel, and proceeded to hack my own voodoo doll to pieces.

I don't think it worked. Maybe I should have kept practicing.

My mother continued to drive me nuts. After a while, I stopped trying to please her. I have only one memory from my entire youth of feeling close to her. I was six. She bathed me and wrapped me in a warm towel. I still remember that moment. I wished there were more. I loved her, of course. That's what children do. But nowhere is it written that it is one's duty to love a parent. It wasn't until years later that I learned that to be loved, you must be loving. Love has to be deserved and earned, by everyone. My father knew this. My mother?

"Let's send the boy to a shrink," she finally said, removing herself and Captain Smug from any responsibility for my rebelliousness at home and in school.

Consider Where
the Joke That Goes Too Far
Might Take You

The office of Maurice Cohn, my first psychiatrist, was located in White Plains, about a half-hour drive from our home. Mother sent me in a taxicab. I had the same driver for each trip: Ray. He was from Tunisia, a fascinating part of the world I itched to explore, the North African home of belly dancers, camel caravans, and, apparently, venereal diseases.

"They put this thing down your dick and scrape," he told me about remedying syphilis. A rather strange admission to a stranger, especially one who was a young boy, and especially to a young boy en route to a shrink. But it was an introduction to another aspect of sexual activity, a subject that was beginning to fascinate me increasingly.

The interior of Dr. Cohn's office on the second floor was bizarre. The walls were covered in Rorschach drawings, and around the room were stick figures. This was creepy shit.

I hated every minute of so-called therapy. The sessions were on Friday afternoons—the same time as baseball practice. I was the pitcher on the team, a crucial position that I loved, and missing practice was a big deal, especially on a regular basis. Naturally, this was the time my mother chose to schedule me to see Dr. Cohn.

I resented being there. Dr. Cohn was bizarre. He wore cheap blue suits with brown cracked shoes and white sport socks. He had poor hygiene too, and I can still see the blizzard of dandruff falling from his thinning black hair down over his face, landing on both sides of his chubby little nose. As a doctor, he was not impressive. I found him easy to manipulate.

He kept probing me, but I never wanted to give him what he was after. I finally felt sorry for him. I realized he had a dismal practice and an odd personality, and I wondered if he needed a therapist more than I did. I knew he wanted me to be revealing, to make an admission, something he could hang his hat on. Every once in a while, when I gave him a nugget he would scribble down on his pad, he'd let me have the verboten can of Coke and a marshmallow, stuff I loved and certainly didn't get at home. All of my favorite treats had been banned by my mother long ago, precisely because they were my favorites.

One fall afternoon, suffering from sheer boredom and frustration, and wanting to get away from those scary Rorschach drawings and stick figures, I came up with an idea.

"Can we go on a field trip?" I asked eagerly.

"Okay, okay," he said, excited that I might open up to him.

We left his spooky office, walked down the stairs to the sidewalk, and looked around. Across the street was a small patch of grass and a park bench. We crossed through traffic and sat there on the bench. It was a beautiful fall day, the sun was out, and I felt so sorry for this guy. He'd tried hard to crack me. He must have felt like a failure, I thought.

Then a few pigeons strutted by. The autumn light in the crisp air caught their feathers, and I could see the colors shine on their black, purple, and green hackles.

"Isn't that beautiful?" I said, pointing to the resplendent colors in the birds' feathers.

Dr. Cohn got excited. He sensed an opening.

"Tell me, Jonathan, what does that remind you of?" he asked.

It hit me. After giving him nothing for months, I knew what he was fishing for and how to make Maurice Cohn's day. Sitting on the park bench, I turned and gave him the answer he was waiting for.

Three magic words.

"My mother's vagina," I said.

Bingo! He smiled wide, put his arm around my shoulders, and hurried me back to his office. Extra marshmallows and Cokes for all!

Shortly after, content that he had his brilliant diagnosis, he conferred with my mother. I had hoped never to see Maurice Cohn again, and my wish came true. After making my disclosure on pigeon feathers, he had come to the conclusion that I needed a far more serious set of treatments. A lone practitioner like him could not do the job alone. Instead, he recommended to my mother and stepfather that they send me to the Phelps School, a school for "boys like me."

Just Because You Fight Fair Doesn't Mean the World Will Too

The Phelps School was located in a farming town outside of Philadelphia, far from the rest of my family back in New York. It was dedicated to giving personal attention to a range of teenagers others couldn't handle. A bit too personal, I was to find out.

From the outside, the Phelps School looked idyllic enough. As we drove in through the front gates, I saw the austere Tudor building that housed the dorms and classrooms, all surrounded by farmland. The school was only a few years old, the vision of Dr. Norman T. Phelps, whom we met after we arrived. He wore high leather boots, all shined up, had a buzz cut, and carried a riding crop. He looked more like an aide-de-camp to Hitler than an educator.

"Achtung!" he shouted as he greeted me with a handshake, crushing all my fingers. Or at least that's what I thought I heard.

I turned to my mother to politely ask her not to leave me in the company of this Gestapo-like man, but, once again, she was speeding away in her Packard, back to New York. Without me.

"Achtung!" Führer Phelps said again, promptly dispatching me to an aide, who escorted me to my bunk in the dorms. I scanned the other kids, searching for friendly, sympathetic faces. There weren't any. So I introduced myself to an unfriendly-faced upperclassman.

"My name is Jonathan. What's your name?"

"Fritzy." Fritzy looked more like an SS recruiter than a student. He had hair on the back of his fingernails, and my estimate was that he'd reached the complete state of puberty at six months.

"I'm going to keep my eye on you." This was less comforting than it was menacing. I scanned the dorm for a place to get out of sight. Since there was none, I walked straight out the door and continued onto the path and into the cornfields by the road. I kept walking deeper in, so deep that nobody could find me. Eventually, it got dark. Then it got cold. I had no choice: I walked back to Phelps and got in my bunk, far from my father and safety.

Soon, morning came, and I learned that I had been banished not to a reformatory school at all but to a labor camp. I was shown my daily chores: mucking out the horse barns, then into the fields for farmwork. Before classes started. We were then forced to attend chapel and participate in a Christian prayer service. The organ started to play, and we all were ordered to sing in unison.

> *Onward, Christian soldiers,*
> *Marching as to war,*
> *With the cross of Jesus*
> *Going on before.*

What was this? I looked around frantically and found one other wide-eyed student who didn't know the lyrics. Herman Weiss was the only other Jewish kid there, and we looked at each other, perplexed and panicked. We hummed along, fearful of being reprimanded if we were caught not singing.

Christ, the royal master,
Leads against the foe;
Forward into battle
See his banners go!

Back in the dorms, when I could safely use the phone, I called my father. I begged him to pick me up and take me away.

"Hang in there, you can handle it," he told me over the phone.

"Please come get me." My usual refrain.

"I can't," he said.

Legally, he was bound. He and my mother were tangled up in a custody case that was stuck in court. He was trying to win the legal battle, he told me, but that was challenging: His lawyer was a friend he met playing pickup basketball in Harlem. My wealthy stepfather's army of well-heeled attorneys, on the other hand, were headed by General Baron, a man so accomplished at litigation he was called on to establish the legal system in the territory of Guam. Seriously. The entire legal system of Guam.

My father encouraged me to stay tough. Things would change as I got older, he told me, and he was doing all he could, and he promised he would keep fighting for me. I knew he was. He was just severely outgunned.

Know When to Make an Exit

In every direction at Phelps, there were threats. Mr. Arnold, the name I'll use for one of the teachers, was a cause for imminent concern. At night, he'd hold the boys on his lap and tell them bedtime stories. These bedtime stories were quite interactive, complete with hands on thighs and other places. But they paled in significance to my biggest threat there: Fritzy. He wasn't the smartest adolescent giant, just an aspiring Neanderthal, and everyone was afraid of him because he ran the circle jerks, whether we wanted to partake or not.

The circle jerks took place in the barn, before the evening prayers. Fritzy tapped the Hogan brothers, a host of other kids, and myself to meet him there. We stood around the hay bales, jacking off in front of one another. It wasn't the worst part of the day, certainly better than Christian prayers. Can I be honest? I kind of liked the experience. I felt like I had something in common at last with my contemporaries at Phelps, like I belonged to this secret group of brothers, albeit a secret group of brothers who masturbated in front of one another. Maybe things were looking up. That is, until I learned that Fritzy and the others were, at best, anti-Semites and, more likely, full-blown aspiring Nazi sympathizers.

Perhaps a lot of this was in my imagination. Then again, the neatly drawn swastikas on all of Fritzy's notebooks were very, very real. Granted, he was also pretty good at drawing the Star of David. The problem was he usually superimposed said star on the unfortunate fellow in the game of hangman. One day he did this in class. He sketched the body parts, branded the figure with the religious six-sided shape, then pointed at me. He then drew an arrow at the hanged man's chest. And smiled. So much for my imagination. It was time to go.

I was afraid to escape from Phelps by myself. In plotting my escape, I needed a partner: My lone fellow tribesman seemed to be the best candidate. If he could be convinced, I thought, Herman Weiss and I might have a chance to break free. Also, if we were caught, it might be harder for Führer Phelps to get away with too much punishment if there were two of us in the school brig.

To convince my compatriot, I told Herman to meet me at my hiding spot in the cornfields, a place where we could talk and Fritzy and the others could not hear us.

Herman wasn't having it.

"If we break out of school, how would we get home?" he asked me. "We have no money."

"Look, we could die here," I said urgently. "We might not make it if we stay. They'd never know the truth." Even then I had a flair for the dramatic.

Herman was nervous, worried about the punishment.

"Have fun with Fritzy," I said. "I'm going. With you or without you."

"How do we get on the train?" he argued. "We don't have any money."

"We hide in the bathroom," I said. "I do it all the time going to see my father." This was an old trick I and other runaways often used to avoid the conductors. In those days, the train bathrooms were nicely appointed and usually had a bench, which came in handy, as I was tired from my escape.

"But what if our parents take us back here? They'd really punish us."

"What do you call this?" I said, and went into another fib to push Herman over the edge. I paused for emphasis and affected deep concern.

"What if they never found your body, Herman?"

He paled.

"And another thing—I didn't want to tell you . . ."

"What?"

"I overheard something in Mr. Arnold's class," I said.

"Wha-wha-what's that?" Herman stammered fearfully.

I took a long, deep breath and looked over my shoulder to make sure no spies were around. In my most conspiratorial voice I shared some crucial and wholly fabricated news.

"Fritzy is planning our execution."

"I never liked Fritzy."

"No shit," I said. "We might not get another chance. Now, here's the deal: Yom Kippur is next week."

Yom Kippur, the Jewish Day of Atonement, was the perfect

cover for Herman and me to escape our captors. A few weeks before, I'd called my father, knowing as always that I could count on him, and asked him to encourage the headmaster, Phelps, to get us to a synagogue, it being so important to our family of nonpracticing atheists. I knew even Führer Phelps could not refuse this kind of religious request. My plan worked. On the morning of Yom Kippur, Phelps's driver picked us up in the headmaster's woody station wagon, and off we went to shul.

The synagogue was half an hour away in the town of West Chester, Pennsylvania. We walked inside, put on our yarmulkes, and scanned the room for exits. I ducked inside the men's bathroom. At the far corner, I noticed a window. I jumped to grab the windowsill, pulled myself up, and looked out. Freedom! Outside, I saw scaffolding. The synagogue was under renovation and getting a fresh coat of paint.

The scaffolding and all the painting equipment were perfect cover, and our very own ladder to freedom. I went to fetch Herman.

"I got a spot," I told him. "This is our chance. Let's go."

Herman followed me into the bathroom. I pointed toward the window and boosted him up until he could get his grip and wriggle his fat ass through. Splat. I heard him land on the sidewalk. I hoped he was still ambulatory. Then I jumped, pulling myself up and squeezing out. My dress shoes landed on the sidewalk. I steadied myself and pulled Herman to his feet, and we ran for it.

Once the synagogue was safely out of sight behind us, we slowed down to catch our breath, wandering through the suburban cul-de-sacs until we found a main road. After an hour or so passed, we arrived at Christie's, a diner on the edge of the expressway. It was attached to a truck stop, and the rigs we passed as we walked onto the property had license plates from all over the country. My father had sent me five dollars for my birthday, so we walked inside the diner and ordered the perfect celebratory meal for the Jewish day of fasting: bacon, breakfast sausage, and pancakes. It wasn't until we had finished that we realized we had a problem: We'd spent most of our money and had only a measly dollar apiece left.

Herman was quiet. I assuaged him with a piece of chocolate cake.

"How do we get home?" he said.

"Why do we want to go home?" I said.

Looking at the trucks in the parking lot, I had another idea.

"Let's hop a truck," I said. "We can sneak on, right in the back."

Herman began sweating.

"We could fall off," he said.

"Yeah, and we could also get tied up by Fritzy and hanged," I said, standing up. "You want to go back there?"

Herman shook his head, traces of chocolate frosting on his lips.

"You with me?" I asked, boldly enough to show I was ready to find our ride to freedom in the parking lot but not brave enough to go by myself.

"How do we know where the truck is going?" Herman said.

"Who gives a shit?"

"We could end up in California," he whined.

"So?" I said. "The farther away from Phelps, the better. You want to sit on Mr. Arnold's lap again for another bedtime story? They probably have the Dobermans out looking for us now. Someone is going to give us up any minute. Let's get out of here."

We scrambled up from the booth, Herman stopping momentarily to shovel the last forkful of chocolate cake into his mouth, and scampered out into the parking lot. Most of the freighters were closed up, except for one decrepit vegetable truck. I jumped up in the back, turned around, and pulled Herman aboard. We crawled around the back, taking refuge amid the crates of produce.

The engine soon rumbled and the back of the trailer started to shake. The vegetable truck pulled out, and we found ourselves on the highway. It was cold and windy in the back of the truck, and without any money or warm clothes, we prayed we were not on the long trip to California after all. Our prayers were answered an hour later—sort of—when we pulled into Wilmington, Delaware. We jumped out, found our way to the bus station, snuck on a bus to Philadelphia, and then boarded a train.

Serendipitously for Herman, the train stopped in Camden, New Jersey, where his family was based. He'd had enough. I wasn't as fortunate. I was homeless, as far as I was concerned. I couldn't go back to Phelps and face Fritzy and the Führer. I also couldn't go back to where the trouble had started for me: my mother and stepfather's home in Westchester. I had only one refuge: my father. I wanted to live with him and have him be my sole guardian.

The train continued on to New York and I snuck into the bathroom.

I was discovered by the conductors, but they were very understanding. Positive Phelps had put out an all-points bulletin that I was gone, I concocted a story that my mother was on her last legs in a Midtown hospital and I was very upset that the school wouldn't allow me to go until I was picked up by an adult the next day. They admired my spunk and compassion. One even bought me a sandwich and a Coke and gave me two dollars, just in case.

After several hours in a train bathroom, I was very glad to reach New York. I walked around Times Square in awe of the sights, the peep shows, the hookers, and the smut shops. I bought three hamburgers at White Castle and two hot dogs at Nedick's. I don't think it all cost more than a buck. Feeling like a grown-up, enjoying my freedom, I stopped into the automat for a nickel cup of coffee. Lots of cream.

I called my father, but he wasn't in. I hoped he wasn't away fishing. I wondered how my mother and stepfather were handling my being on the lam again. Maybe now they were sorry for sending me away to Phelps. That psychiatrist had really screwed up my life with those damn pigeons, I thought. Then it occurred to me that, just maybe, I was partly to blame for having said what I said.

I guess they thought I was really disturbed. I know they thought I held certain proclivities and could end up as a pervert. After all, I frequently tried to watch One-Eyed Betty undress through the blinds. And my stepfather's sister, on the occasions when I would spend the night at her house. Maybe they were onto something. I remembered, years earlier, proudly marching around Aunt Estelle's house with my hairy and voluptuous cousin's bloomers over my head. I was five. Some kids like yo-yos. Some like model planes. I liked scented panties. There was just something amazing about them.

I kept calling Pop but got no answer, so I decided to take the subway up to Eighty-Sixth Street and wait him out at his place.

It was then that I spotted a deck of cards with naked ladies on them in a smut shop window. I decided they were worth my remaining money and foregoing the subway for a hell of a long walk to Pop's.

He still wasn't home. I fell asleep on the doorstep. When I woke up, I was hungry and I was chilly. In my desperate state, I started to consider Scarsdale. Maybe by this time they would have started to miss me. I might gain a few points by running to them instead of my father's. (They didn't have to know I had already tried and failed.) Maybe they'd see I was finally coming to my senses, ready to be the "good," manageable boy they wanted, ready to join their happy home at last.

Deluded into this fantasy, I hid out on the last commuter train. These were always easy because they were crowded: Even if the bathroom was busy, you could simply walk up and down the aisles. As long as you never sat down, they'd never have the opportunity to ask you for a ticket.

I arrived and walked another two miles home from the railroad station. Phelps, the shul, Christie's Diner, Delaware, all seemed like ages ago. I planned to be nice and sweet. I knew One-Eyed Betty would be glad to see me and feed me the stuff I liked. She was pissed at them anyway for sending away her drinking partner.

I walked in just as a barbecue was wrapping up. My stepfather had a gaggle of business big shots assembled. He glared at me. My mother, much to my surprise, seemed concerned. Or at least she appeared to be. She gave me a hug. I liked that. It didn't happen often. She told me Phelps had called in the morning and she was really worried but thought I was with my father.

My stepfather finally tore himself away from his associates and cornered me in the kitchen. He was upset. Really upset. It was more than just the embarrassment of me arriving in the middle of dinner. Was it possible that he cared a little after all?

I took the opening. I told him and my mother, in no uncertain terms, that if I was sent back to Phelps I would jump off the top of the silo on parents' day. They looked at each other, comprehension of my precipitous state finally dawning on them.

I was sent back to Phelps the very next day.

Never Let School Get in the Way of Your Education

Fate intervened before I did my swan dive off the highest point at Phelps. One rainy, gray November morning, the headmaster called me into his office and told me news that burst through the gloom of the day like a ray of sunshine:

My stepfather had had a nervous breakdown.

I was told to pack my things, and the next day I not only left Phelps behind forever but also left the Northeast for a time. We—my mother, my recently adopted younger sister, and my stepfather—were on our way to Florida, where my stepfather could rest. The drive was scenic and quiet, which suited me fine. The only happening of note over the thousands of miles of road was at a rest stop in North Carolina.

There, in the bathroom, was a condom machine. I couldn't believe it. I stuffed my only coins into the machine and marveled at my newly acquired and now most prized possession. I put it in my pocket and we continued on our way.

. . .

Once we were in Florida, my path was clear. I was going to be a pearl diver. I was ten, maybe eleven. While I had a vague awareness that the best oyster beds were located in the Philippines and around the emirates on the Red Sea, and the pearl divers in these far-flung locales could descend to more than a hundred feet below sea level in one dive by holding their breath for more than seven minutes, I had to start my training in the body of water closest to me: the main pool of the Fontaine-bleau Hotel.

I still remember the smell of suntan lotion, surf, and grease from the grill that hung in the humid air of southern Florida, a place where we didn't live for very long. In the 1950s, the Fontainebleau had just opened, and the incredible panoramic face of the hotel and epic sweep of rooms quickly became a hangout for an eclectic mix of clientele: drug smugglers, wannabe gangsters, and an entrenched population of Jewish bubbes and zaydes betting their nickels and quarters playing games like mah-jongg and canasta all afternoon under the umbrellas by the pool. This pool was special. It had been designed to look like a tropical lagoon, lined with the rattling fronds of palm trees and complete with its own waterfall. The hotel had been designed by Morris Lapidus and was built like a time-travel machine. "If you create a stage and it is grand, everyone who enters will play their part," he said.

Jimmy Schwaab was another scrawny kid from New York who had come to the Fontainebleau with his family on vacation; he was like a child vacuum cleaner. Jimmy had developed a fool-proof way to collect a percentage of the change the cabal of grandmothers were churning around the mah-jongg tables. His ruse was simple: He pretended to be a native pearl diver, but instead of grabbing pearls, he asked the yentas to throw their spare change into the pool and he would dive in after it. When I saw all the shining change that Jimmy had been making, I asked to join forces with him.

Together, we worked the Fontainebleau pool in the mornings and afternoons—you know, the times when I should have been in school. On my first day, after going home, I counted all my newfound fortune on my bed. I couldn't believe how much I'd made. More than ten dollars! Those earnings were far more than any other job had paid or any other allowance I'd received.

Business was so good for Jimmy and me that we figured we could recruit a team of divers to work with us and take a percentage of their earnings. We could even expand operations to other resorts and pools. Heck, we were so good in the water, holding our breath and acting like natives, we could start our own salvage company and find buried treasure, diving for gold coins among the wrecks off Key Biscayne and Bimini. Sadly, we never got our operation together. After the third day, we closed up shop. Jimmy had to go back to New York.

As for me, I came home to find my mother in tears. What had I done? Well, for starters, I hadn't bothered to go to school once, and the principal had called. But that wasn't all. I looked down at my sister. She was playing with a small balloon. But it wasn't a balloon. It was a condom, inflated and tied off.

My condom. The one I'd purchased in North Carolina.

"How could you do this?" my mother wailed.

Here's the thing, which I didn't realize until much later. My little sister was three. How could she have opened the condom package, let alone blown it up into a balloon and tied it off so deftly? She'd had help. And I believe the culprit was the one standing over her with tears in her eyes, asking me how I could do this. She should know.

It didn't matter. I listened through the door as my mother spoke to my father from the other room.

"Milton, I can no longer handle the boy. I'm sending him to you immediately."

That afternoon, I landed with my bag at LaGuardia Airport and walked out onto the tarmac. My father was waiting in his gym shoes, standing up to his ankles in new-fallen snow. There were no pools around here. My career as a pearl diver was over. I never even snagged a pearl, but I discovered a jewel of wisdom under the waters of the Fontainebleau lagoon. A lot of nickels and dimes can add up quickly to dollars, but only if you're willing to go out and get them.

Some Rites of Passage Aren't Right at All

My journey to manhood continued to be transient. I would spend months intermittently with my father, then with my mother and stepfather, then with my father again. At least I convinced them never to return me to Phelps. My mother and stepfather left Florida again for tony Westchester County, outside of New York City. I toughed it out with them for stretches at my father's behest.

My new high school in Yorktown Heights wasn't as abusive as the Phelps School, but I struggled to find anyone like me. The students had farmers as parents. My background, of course, was very different. But I wanted to fit in, like all kids do. I wanted to be popular, and to do so, as any kid knows, you have to befriend other popular students. I found my cool mentor in the only other Jewish kid in school. He was Anthony Hatzenberg, but he went by a different name. Everyone called him Tony Mambo Tony.

For the 1950s, Tony Mambo Tony was the epitome of hip.

The rage was pink, and he was decked out in pink socks, pink pop-collar shirts, pink ties. Everyone called him Tony Mambo Tony because even before his own bar mitzvah he was an extraordinary dancer. He played the congas and bongos and was so talented he sat in with the great Tito Puente at the Palladium in New York City. He was shorter than me, with a head of jet-black hair he greased back for performances. I remember watching him on the stage, sporting his sunglasses, hands a blur on the drums, just looking off to the side and lost in his own jazzy euphoria. Tony Mambo Tony was the coolest thing on two feet, I thought. So did he.

Tony's parents had come from the city—he spent weekends there—so we spoke the same language. Through his connections with Latin musicians, a group of bona fide adults who were not our parents, Tony Mambo Tony had the keys to the real world, a place that many of us randy teenagers at Yorktown knew little about.

"You want to get laid?" he asked.

"Yeah," I said, eager to end my virginity and declare myself a man.

"I got a great hooker."

"Okay! What's her name?"

"Edie. Edie Matthews."

"What's the deal?"

"I'll set it all up," he said.

As I waited for the date, I practiced in my room, trying on condoms after my mother and Lippe had gone to sleep, familiarizing myself with how to get them on and off like a pro. I'd want to appear experienced. It was winter, and after making the first cut of the junior varsity basketball team, I recruited my teammates to accompany me down to see Edie. When the day came, we all hopped in my car, drinking beer and lying about everything we'd ever done or knew.

"Oh man, I hear she's a great fuck," one of the guys said, as if he'd had dozens of conquests, but I suspected they were virgins like me.

"She's Puerto Rican," someone else said as we continued down the West Side Highway.

I was the driver in my stepfather's Packard. I remembered One-Eyed Betty's warning: Be careful with that little thing of yours. I thought of Ray, the old taxi driver from Tunisia who regaled me with the tales of his own venereal diseases, and thought about putting on a second condom for extra protection. The braggadocio and bravado diminished as we got closer to ground zero. Once we arrived, Tony Mambo Tony made the call and we all piled into the building. I looked up the stairs. On the third-floor landing, a man opened the door to size us up. His gold tooth glinted in the dull light, a large Doberman at his side. Must have been the pimp, I thought.

"Come on up, boys," he said in accented English, as the sound of a dozen trepidatious feet climbed.

Waiting in the hallway, we found a half dozen students from Princeton, wearing their varsity jackets and smoking pipes. We got in line, waiting for our turn. We were so cool.

I was standing next to Tony Mambo Tony.

"Tone, what do I tell her?" I asked nervously, searching for a few tips, making sure the others didn't hear.

"Kid, it's easy. You sit on the edge of the bed and say, 'Edie, honey, I'm new at this game. You've got to show me the ropes.'"

The lines were good. I repeated them to myself, committing them to memory.

"You'll be fine," he said. We chose between us, and I got to go first.

I walked in the room. The first thing I saw was a cross nailed to the wall above the bed. Oh good, I thought. Edie Matthews is a religious girl.

"Let's go, baby," she said. "I'm busy. I got people."

Edie was pretty enough. She was wearing a long T-shirt that covered her thighs and had long red hair and long red fingernails to match. She was skinny, underfed, but beautiful to me. I tried to talk with her, ask her a few questions and get to know her.

She complained about her bladder. She had internal problems, she said, and needed an operation. Her womb was tilted or something. It sounded serious. She'd need money for it and, well, my five dollars was supporting the cause. She then reached her hand into a giant tub of Vaseline, lifted up her legs, and rubbed it in the general area of concern.

I took off my clothes and she removed her T-shirt and lay back. I sat on the bed, which was covered in damp T-shirts, and delivered the magic lines Tony Mambo Tony had fed me.

"Edie, honey, I'm new at this game," I said. "You've got to show me the ropes."

"No problem, baby," she said. "Get on top of me."

I did just that. With her scrawny naked body in front of me, I collapsed into her embrace. She reached down, grabbed my twice-protected little thing, and placed me inside her.

I started moving around, pretending I knew what I was doing, rocking my head back. Yeah, this was it, I thought. But it didn't feel special at all. Something was wrong.

"What's the matter?" Edie said.

"I can't feel anything," I said.

"You've got that thing on," she said, instantly identifying the source of the problem. "You don't need no rubber with me. I'm clean."

Visions of the Princeton varsity team, all seven guys before me, flashed into view. Either way, I was desperate for my first experience to be special, and despite all better judgment and thoughts of Ray's and One-Eyed Betty's warnings, I removed my condoms and entered what felt like a primordial soup. I felt powerful. I had done it. I had achieved something special. Edie Matthews, bless her, had made me a man.

Or so I thought. Even minutes later, driving back upstate in the now quiet and lacking-in-bravado car, feeling like the captain of our basketball team for what I had done, something didn't feel right. Yes, I had lost my virginity and conquered that rite of passage. But was the test of manhood the actual act of sex, a carnal experience that carried little meaning, or the intimacy and specialness that can come along with it? It would take me years to discover that such an act, something so physical, was infinitely more real when paired with something emotional. In the end, I concluded that Edie was an illusion. She wasn't my gateway to manhood. She wasn't really my gateway to anything.

If Being You Isn't Working, Be Someone Else

I was always short—not just in stature. (In fact, there was at least one time when I was too tall.) No, I was always short on cash. For spending money, I worked a variety of jobs. I had a paper route. I stocked a liquor store upstate. I even worked at a Christmas tree farm not too far from Sing Sing, and perhaps on the same power grid. Whenever they would execute somebody, the lights on our Christmas trees would grow dim. The moment had come to find a better way to spend my time.

It was the late 1950s, and I ventured deep into the Catskills, accepting a position at Gibber's, a hotel, and quickly earning the title of the world's worst busboy. I was so inept, they would only let me wait on the unimportant guests and the Gibber's family— who lacked in manners what I lacked in proficiency as a server. The kitchen was a mess, the owners were cheap, and they never fed us enough. I was always hungry, and cleaning off all the un-eaten brisket, gefilte fish, and herring created a painful rumbling in my stomach. If I saw an untouched piece, I'd grab it before dumping it into the trash, give a fake sneeze, and inhale it.

Scraps weren't enough, however. I was a growing young man, fresh out of high school. Always hungry, I came up with a ruse. At some point in the night, I'd go to the chef and ask to take out a plate for Mr. Schwartz. The chef would hand me the plate, but instead of going into the dining room to deliver the meal to a seated guest, I went down the hall and into the card room. Here, in the corner, was a giant boxy old television set. I'd place Mr. Schwartz's dinner in the back, hiding it in the empty space next to the television's tubes. Mr. Schwartz never had a chance to eat his dinner. But I did. I was Mr. Schwartz.

One day, there was a big baseball game on. I scrambled through the kitchen and approached the chef.

"Special order for Mr. Schwartz," I said, then returned to pick up a gorgeous plate of duck the chef had prepared and hid the delicacy in my hiding spot.

That day, the Yankees were playing, and a number of guests had retreated to the card room to watch the game. The reception on the television wasn't working; the screen was dusted over in black-and-white static. The handyman was called to fix it. He went around the back to jigger the tubes and discovered Mr. Schwartz's succulent duck with the crispy skin that I had secreted away.

Mr. Schwartz and I were fired on the spot.

I was better off anyway. Those bosses were cheap, and there was no sense in wasting time working for bosses who didn't treat their staff well.

Flexibility Isn't Just for Gymnasts

Banished from Gibber's, I was now a free agent on the busboy circuit. Acting on a tip from inside the kitchen, I drove over to Ted Hilton's Hideaway, a resort in Moodus, Connecticut. It was a magnificent resort, known then as a place where wealthy, flirtatious older women came to get attention from the camp's young, virulent, hustling staff. Again, I worked in the kitchen. I was the salad man, a position that, despite the moniker "man," was indeed lower on the career ladder than busboy. My first day on the job, I stuffed two thousand prunes with peanut butter.

I didn't last long. I was caught leaving the cabin of one of the resort's guests. This wasn't a punishable infraction. In fact, it was to be expected, almost part of the job. But this particular guest was also the mistress of the resort owner.

I was fired on the spot. Again.

Back to the Catskills. This time, I was accepted for work at

Laurel in the Pines, a major resort in Monticello. Hired as a bus-boy, I reported for duty immediately in the kitchen and was given my orders to clean up the dining room. This place was massive. I scrambled around, getting lost in the kitchen.

"Excuse me, you know where the dining room is?" I asked one of the staff, an older gentleman. He turned out to be the head maître d', a fussy old bag who wondered how a busboy could get lost in the kitchen and fail to locate the dining room.

Again, fired on the spot.

I was running out of resorts. Up near Lake George, in the Adirondacks, I found Sven and Margaret Monk's motel. Here I was hired as a waiter, an upgrade from busboy, and was making decent tips. I brought Mr. Schwartz with me—he seemed to trail me wherever I went—so I was getting fed. Best of all, I had a side hustle that netted me a little extra.

The Saratoga racetrack was close. Every day, some buddies and I would place bets on horses for the guests and drive down to register their orders at the track. Most of the time, regardless of what the guests asked us to bet, we'd place their money on the favorites. When their horses lost, we could report the grim news, while having a good chance of walking away with some winnings ourselves. It was the perfect plot. The only way we could lose is if the chalk horses failed and a long shot won. But that wasn't going to happen.

Until it did. Three times. In one day. With a limited bank, I was out of the bookmaking business. At least I still had my waiting job.

It was during lunch one day when a woman strutted in wear-ing furs. She looked like a grand old dame, with her chauffeur in full livery. She sat down at a table.

"Waiter, waiter, this is too much ice," she said, pointing at her water glass.

"Oh, waiter, is this butter?" she went on, after I had replaced her butter with butter.

"Waiter, this is too salted."

"Waiter, this is rather bland."

Never happy. Just like my mother.

Finally, her coffee came out, and I placed the mug in front of her.

"Waiter, waiter," she said, pointing to the cup. "Is this milk or is this cream?"

"I don't know, toots," I said, jamming my finger into the cup and then licking it.

"Cream," I declared with a grin.

Fired on the spot.

I left the next morning, embracing the open road and the adventures that lay ahead. Heading back north, I passed through Ausable Chasm, a picturesque natural gorge in the Adirondacks, and saw a construction site. I got out, inquired about work, and, much to my surprise, was hired immediately. I was a laborer, and I helped the others who were building a bridge across the gorge. The heat was unbearable, hanging onto a jackhammer shook my brain loose, and the sound of the dynamite blasts rattled my body.

Within hours, I deserved some R and R. Next to the site was a house with a swimming pool. From the back fence, I threw a handful of stones into the water. I then went around to the front of the house and knocked on the front door.

A woman answered.

"I'm so sorry," I said, and then went into the most elaborate lie about how the dynamite blasts had accidentally launched a few stones into her pool. I graciously volunteered to retrieve them, happily stripped to my skivvies, and dove in to get them out, deliberately taking the time to meticulously collect every last stone.

I didn't last long on my construction job, but for once my departure wasn't performance related. I was living in a motel and wound up flirting with the receptionist. Two days later, her boyfriend appeared. With a shotgun. He asked me to leave town, an invitation I quickly accepted.

I was back on the road again. But I had my trout rod with me, and I would stop, camp out, and fish. The lost jobs didn't concern me. I had my adventures, my reels and rods. What I lacked in ambition, I easily made up for in contentment.

But I was hungry.

Eventually, I packed it all up and went to college.

Don't Be Overconfident
If You're Going to Underdeliver

I attended junior college at Boston University—I didn't have the grades to get into the main school—where I majored in gin rummy and minored in dog handicapping at Wonderland Dog Track. I was lost without a hero like my father to follow. During my first semester, I found him. Or should I say her. Her name was Texas Yellow Rose, and she was one of the greatest racing dogs I'd ever seen. Texas Yellow Rose was never the favorite at the Wonderland track in Revere. But she frequently came from behind, closed tremendously, and won. The dog was miraculous. She was moving up in class; she was on her way, and I was with her. I went to the track and after entrance fees had enough for one two-dollar daily-double ticket. I placed my hopes on her, so convinced she would win. The race was thrilling. I went hoarse screaming. Texas Yellow Rose, my champion, came back from behind the pack just like always when she was closing toward the finish line.

She lost by a photo finish. I nearly had a heart attack. I would have won seven hundred dollars on the two-dollar bet. I went home empty-handed and hungry.

I felt like that dog, always trying to come from behind but never being great enough. I seldom went to class. Instead, I glued myself to the windowsill of my dorm with a few hundred other students, angling for the view across the street.

She must have known we were watching. She'd undress herself, leaving the blinds open just so and driving us all raving mad. She was a voyeur's dream, kept by a high-ranking military man who must have been on a mission that fall, and every night she'd put on a show. We all fantasized about her and came up with all kinds of schemes to win her heart or at least get her number. There was more than a hundred bucks in the pot for the first guy lucky enough to bed her.

By chance one day I saw her in a Laundromat around the corner. I ducked in, pretended to need instruction on one of the machines, and made small talk with her. She was more beautiful up close, and I was enthralled, seeing in my mind's eye all those nights I'd watched her undress in the window. I immediately got this spasm in my back that always occurred when I was acutely aroused.

"You look familiar," I said, knowing full well that I'd seen every part of her body and made her the focal point of every fantasy I'd had since arriving at school. When she told me she lived nearby, I acted surprised and suggested we have a glass of wine together later that night.

"I like red," she said.

I arrived at her building a few hours later, entered an apartment I already knew, and looked back at my dorm to see a raucous crowd spilling over one another at the windowsill and pointing in my direction. I had made the ultimate collegiate fantasy come true. I had entered the lair of our sexy exhibitionist neighbor. I was so proud of myself. Glancing around the apartment, I looked for pictures of her high-ranking boyfriend, a sergeant or perhaps even a colonel, who could surely cripple me in his grip. It felt dangerous to be in that space, sharing a glass of red with his vixen. The adrenaline was intoxicating.

Soon enough, we were in the throes of ecstasy and were squirming around on the bed. I guided her into view so that all my friends across the street could witness my masterful conquest, sure I'd become a rich hero, winning more than a hundred dollars in the pot. But more important, I'd be a legend at BU junior college. I struggled to get her pants off, the cuffs sticking on her high heels. I went on to kiss her body, exhilarated to learn that I could make a grown woman moan. I was her master. I owned her. We moved with breathless abandonment. She was hot. She was wet. I climbed on top of her.

Her lips were next to my ear, her panting breath tickling me. I couldn't believe myself. I couldn't wait to brag to everyone.

Ecstatic over my accomplishment, I showed her some of my very best moves. The secret ones. The ones I reserved for so very few. I wasn't a stud. I was a superstud.

"Honey, baby," she whispered, so close to my ear.

"Yes?" I said, continuing my moves as if I'd committed the *Kama Sutra* to memory.

"Put it in," she said.

Oh my God. Put it in? I thought that I *was* in. I don't know where I was.

Finally, she helped me find the spot. I put it in. Then the show was all over. I was premature. I was ashamed and embarrassed. I left my playmate there on the bed shortly after, unsatisfied and alone.

Back at the dorm, I gave everyone the requisite high fives. I was the hero, and a rich one at that.

"She was a great fuck," I said, standing tall and exaggerating every part of the story over a few beers. But I knew the truth. If I was going to improve my performance, I'd have to practice. And maybe even get some help.

Put All Your Baggage
to Good Use

Somehow, I walked away with an associate of arts degree, but just barely. I hadn't bothered to send out any résumés. In truth, I didn't imagine my life would go on very long. Why waste my precious limited time on a career?

My father was worried about me. Through a random encounter with a new acquaintance, whose details I promised not to divulge, my father developed a connection to Dr. Fredric Wertham, the famed psychiatrist. He'd studied in all the leading schools, even worked with Sigmund Freud, and was esteemed by the medical and educational community. In the 1950s, Wertham authored the popular and controversial book *Seduction of the Innocent,* making a case that violent comic books were instilling children with sociopathic thoughts in their developmental period and creating a new generation of criminals. Dr. Wertham was a national figure, vigorously loathed by the comic book industry and maligned by smut merchants. He still handled a few patients. Among his list of new challenges: me.

His office was dark and quiet, and I sat in front of his desk, inspecting him. He had a lantern face, dark-framed glasses, and a corduroy sport jacket. He scribbled on a pad, an unlit cigarette always dangling from his lips. I was on the couch, he sat behind me. I wondered if he was listening to me at all. From time to time he would clear his throat.

"Ahem," he'd say, writing another note and fingering his cigarette.

Then I told him about Phelps and our circle jerks with Fritzy in the barn before evening prayers.

"Ahem," he'd say, not even looking up at me.

I was really doubting that he was even paying attention, when he perked up in his chair. The great doctor had made a determination.

"Your stepfather is a stinker," he said. "Your mother, I feel sorry for her."

Okay. Thanks, Doc.

Then I told him about my last shrink, twelve years before, the schlub Cohn, to whom I'd declared that a pigeon's feathers had reminded me of my mother's vagina. Wertham's usual expressionless demeanor was broken by a very large smile, which turned into a guffaw of such consequence that the unlit cigarette was expelled from his mouth.

"I want you to come back next week," Wertham said with a devious twinkle in his eye. "There is somebody I want you to meet."

I returned the following week, and waiting in Wertham's office was a man named Philip something or other. He looked most unusual. He was tall and lean, wore a beret and Coke-bottle eyeglasses, and smoked a cigarette from a holder. He had a deep voice like a jazz singer. He invited me to attend a rehearsal at the Living Theatre.

I didn't want to be an actor. I had no interest. My mother had been interested in gardening and design. My father dabbled in watercolor. But acting? For me? No.

Wertham insisted I go. In fact, he stated, it was to be a prerequisite if I wished to continue treatment.

And so I halfheartedly followed Philip what's his name back to the theater on Fourteenth and Sixth Avenue. Philip, as it turned out, was Philip Deacon, a teacher at the Living Theatre and a highly regarded off-Broadway director. The theater was on the cutting edge, at the forefront of all avant-garde theater in the country. They were doing Ionesco and William Carlos Williams. The Living Theatre was dynamic and experimental.

"The best way to deal with yourself as an actor is to follow the emotional truth of the circumstances given to you. And as you develop your technique, you come to believe in what you're doing and trust it because you re-create it emotionally." I was intrigued. Inside the theater, a class was under way. I sat next to Philip, and we both watched as the director onstage worked with a handful of aspiring talents. He invited me to come onstage.

I walked up and stood in front of him. He wanted me to perform an improvisation, a performance without a script. I could do whatever I wanted.

"Okay, here is your dilemma," the director told me. "You're carrying a very heavy suitcase across the desert. The reason the suitcase is so heavy is that inside the suitcase is a fortune of stolen money. You have to make a decision. Should you drop the suitcase and make it out of the desert alive? Or do you decide to lug the suitcase through the arid heat and see if you can survive? Got it?"

"I guess . . . ," I said.

"Action!" the director called, and like that, I was left there alone on the stage, forced to perform the scene. I was uncomfortable. I was in front of a small crowd of strangers. I had nothing to do but fully commit myself to the emotional choices swirling through my mind.

When I had finished, I looked around. The entire class was standing and clapping. I could see smiles on all their faces. I had made them happy. I had done something extraordinary, and it felt so natural. The applause alone was intoxicating. I knew from that moment that my life would never be the same. With this approval, achieved for the first time, and on my own, I'd found my calling—with a little help from Dr. Wertham and Philip Deacon. Introductions to people who can help you are critical, but knowing how to handle them properly can change your life.

Hunger Is the Best Chef

I found an apartment a few blocks away from the United Nations, on Forty-Eighth Street. The apartment was tiny. And infested. We'd turn on the lights and the rooms would positively quiver. I moved in with John Phillip Law, a fellow acting student, and the rent was forty dollars each. He was tall, about six foot five, with blond hair. He would go on to play Pygar, the blind angel in *Barbarella,* which became a cult film only a few years later.

We suffered together. We were always broke, which also meant we were always hungry. On Saturday afternoons, I revived Mr. Schwartz, and Law and I ventured off into the city to fend the pangs of hunger away. We'd shave, dress up, and head across town to swanky hotels like the Waldorf Astoria. We'd follow the signs to the bar mitzvahs—GOTTLIEB MEZZANINE LEVY FLOOR 6—and mingle with the guests like we belonged. After all, we were actors. Part of the role was stuffing ourselves with blintzes, lox, and whatever else we could grab.

As starving artists, we felt entitled to help ourselves. The arts should be supported, we believed, by local businesses like the supermarket—whether they knew they were supporting the arts or not. John had a long black duster for a coat. His girlfriend at the time, Susan Myers, was very handy. She converted that long black coat of his into a shopping cart for us. On the inside, she sewed elastic straps, then sewed those straps to bags inside the coat. Very nicely organized, I must say. We'd go the market, pretending to shop, stuffing packages of short ribs, pork chops, and quartered chickens inside his coat. Back at the house, as dumpy as it was, we had a small patch of a backyard with a lone, straggly tree, a patch of weeds, and a rusted hibachi. Lighting up the charcoal, we'd have barbecue parties, cooking up our stolen food for our fellow actors.

We never got caught. We must have stolen half a cow and a coop of chickens. Of course it was wrong. I knew that. But we were hungry. And it was undeniable: Those feasts, illicit as they were, always tasted delicious.

Play Nice with Others

Dustin Hoffman and I never got along. That's putting it mildly. In truth, Dusty, as we called him back then, was my nemesis. When I was acting at the Neighborhood Playhouse School of the Theatre in New York and performing in theater, Dusty and I were always competing for parts. We were both on the smaller side, both Jewish, a bit swarthy, and there were only so many roles that we could be cast in and play. We also had such different personalities. He was serious and somber, a student of the craft. I took acting seriously as well, but not the way he did. I was more lighthearted. I enjoyed the camaraderie of many friends inside and outside the theater; I was more socially oriented than Dustin.

We were on the road together. We had been cast in *A Cook for Mr. General.* I had traveled a bit on the summer stock circuit, supporting theater greats like Martha Scott, Orson Bean, and Julia Meade (who later went on to sell refrigerators in television commercials). I had trekked to the Ogunquit Playhouse in Kennebunkport, Maine, and the Dennis Theater in Cape Cod. But these theaters were nothing in comparison to the Forrest Theatre in Philadelphia, by far the largest and most ornate stage I had yet to appear on. This was a pre-Broadway run, during which a production was tried out and fine-tuned before making its way to the Great White Way. The cast included Roland Winters—famous for playing Charlie Chan—Bill Travers, and Dustin Hoffman. Among many others. And me.

The cast was all put up in a hotel by the theater. It was amazing to enter a paid-for hotel room each day after rehearsal, considering what I had been through in the past few years: the ongoing auditions, the turndowns, the rejections. But here I was, now a professional actor on Broadway—well, almost. Unlike other plays, where I'd appear in throwaway parts, I even had a line. I'd rehearsed in front of a mirror, in my mind. "All I did was tap him on the shoulder," I was to say.

Before opening night, I received a telegram at the hotel. It was from my father.

"Twenty-three, a man," he wrote me. "What a wonderful age to be, beginning a career with the promise of real success, handsome, intelligent, outgoing personality, adored—what more could I want? To make people happy or sad—what a wonderful place to be."

A Cook for Mr. General was a comedy. Set in the South Pacific, the plot centered on a military rehab center and a ragtag group of mental misfits stuck there and was similar in spirit to *One Flew Over the Cuckoo's Nest.* Bill Travers, a British actor and the lead, spent most of the play in a colored bonnet, knitting a scarf. Roland Winters played a general suffering from an ulcer. One patient was convinced he was Jesus Christ. Another answered the morning roll call by crowing like a rooster.

I played Sullivan, a soldier, with my single, cherished line. And Dusty played Ridzinski, another misfit soldier. We had been cast onstage and lined up according to height. Army style. I was the second shortest next to Hoffman.

We laughed together only once. In one performance, Roland Winters, the general, was berating all the soldiers for being the degenerate, shell-shocked screw-ups we were. Winters had his back to the audience, and as he was screaming in our faces, the saliva flying, a booger appeared in Winters's nose. And the more he worked himself up into a rage, the bigger the booger got. I struggled to keep in character, starting to smirk. Dusty chortled next to me uncontrollably. Winters was playing furious, but he was also furious with us. He laced into us more seriously, but the angrier he got, the farther the booger descended from his nose, now dangling just above his lip. We just couldn't control ourselves. We burst out laughing, ruining his scene. They dropped the curtain prematurely.

"You little fucks!" Winters screamed, trying to grab us backstage. We were chased around the stage by Charlie Chan.

Preproduction lasted two weeks—long enough for me and Dusty to truly irritate each other as we vied for stage presence. One afternoon, a few of us went to lunch at the Harvey House, a restaurant in downtown Philadelphia that was known to cater to mobsters. We sat there across from each other, rubbing each other the wrong way like we always did. Finally, I snapped. I leaned over the table and pointed my finger at him.

"I know why you don't like me," I bellowed.

He sat there, dumbfounded.

"Because I'm going to make it and you're not," I stated definitively, and I stood up and left the restaurant.

I didn't return to that lunch. But over the next forty years, I would have those words to eat. Dusty, the serious one, went on to become one of the greatest actors of my generation, and rightfully so. He wasn't afraid to step out of the box and find new roles for himself, roles that allowed him to demonstrate his extraordinary ability as an actor. He broke the mold and grew as an artist.

The play closed on Broadway prematurely. Once again, I was out of work.

I proceeded to struggle for bit parts but was pushed along by teachers at the Neighborhood Playhouse. I was soon in front of Elia Kazan, a legend in American drama, and one of my favorite directors.

"He's all wrong," Elia Kazan told David Pressman, my teacher, who'd brought me along to meet the great director of *On the Waterfront,* my favorite American film. I never even had a chance to read for the part. And just like that, not even thirty minutes later, I was back out on the street.

Years later, I did an improvisation with Kazan himself, and I guess I was "all right" that time, because he hired me for voice-over bits in his biographical film *America America.* But at that moment, missing my one shot with my favorite director, I was just wondering how I would ever make it as an actor.

Don't Put It in Writing

I called her Wind Nymph. I kept her letters for all these years, but we really shared only a few nights together. But through her words and correspondence, I fell hopelessly in love. At night, I would hold her envelopes, waiting to open them alone in the apartment that we had rented on Central Park South and where we had planned to spend the rest of our lives together. She wrote:

> *I must have read your letter ten times already. Late last night, I found myself saying "Hello out there" over and over again; and knew then forever the full poignant meaning of that phrase. I went to your letter as I would have gone to your arms . . .*

How delightfully sweet. Okay, how corny. But it was new love, passionate and free of judgment.

Wind Nymph was magical. We first met during rehearsals. The studio was on the Lower East Side, in downtown New York, and around the corner from Ratner's, the deli where my father would often take me for fresh onion rolls, pickles, and pastrami. I'd returned, and with a good part. I'd moved into doing TV and was cast in *Focus*, a major television production developed by NBC, directed by Fielder Cook, and written by Arthur Miller, the great playwright and another of my heroes. Miller came by the set, but I rarely had the chance to spend much time with him. At the studio, he was all business: tall, dark glasses, an intellectual.

The story of *Focus* was a story of anti-Semitism, and I played a heavy. My job was to intimidate the Jews. I laughed off the irony and channeled my inner Fritzy.

Wind Nymph played a nurse. She was an incredible spirit but a terrible actress. We fell for each other during the first break. We were inseparable. She was living in Los Angeles, trying to work her way into film, and had to fly back the next day. She also had a boyfriend. Charles was his name.

We crammed in a full relationship in twenty-four hours. We walked in Central Park, the night filled with the warmth of the coming spring, stardust on our shoulders. I got lost in the constellations of her freckles. She was so sensual and curious and all knowing. When I first saw her on the set, she was always reading something or other. Walking with her, then stopping on park benches to listen, I listened to her read Henry Miller, the great novelist whose books *Tropic of Capricorn* and *Tropic of Cancer* had been censored and banned for their evocative prose. My favorites were some of his passages in the book *Sexus*.

What I want is to open up. I want to know what's inside me. I want everybody to open up . . . I know that underneath the mess everything is marvelous. I'm sure of it.

I didn't want Wind Nymph to leave. But she did. She went back to LA. I reread Henry Miller to bring us closer.

She rises up out of a sea of faces and embraces me, embraces me passionately—a thousand eyes, noses, fingers, legs, bottles, windows, purses, saucers all glaring at us and we in each other's arm oblivious. I sit down beside her and she talks—a flood of talk. Wild consumptive notes of hysteria, perversion, leprosy. I hear not a word because she is beautiful and I love her and now I am happy and willing to die.

I couldn't wait to tell my father about her. I went to see him and Uncle Herbie, boasting that I had discovered the most beautiful, wonderful woman on earth. My Wind Nymph! I told them all about our plans to live together—here in New York, with her in Los Angeles—a perfect arrangement for us to pursue our acting careers and a life with each other.

Her letters arrived often:

Memories of you surround me. I wish so terribly that I could get into my little car and drive fast to where you would be waiting. I am filled with such regrets!

My responses were equally gag-worthy:

I saw you last night, briefly. The fire caressing your hair as you turned in sleep like a lamb tasting the first days of spring. Do you still snore, I wonder? So sweetly—I imagine—like wind whispering through forests of lilacs.

This was getting serious. I started looking for an apartment for us. The quicker I could secure us a place to stay, the faster I could perhaps convince Wind Nymph to come live with me in New York. Finally, after several days, I stumbled on the most charming one-bedroom on Central Park West. Old wooden floors, tall windows, and best of all, what I craved the most and what city apartments seldom had: a fireplace. I put down the deposit and wrote to her immediately. She didn't miss a beat:

Late last night before turning out the light I snuggled deep in my covers and opened it to read once again, that I might go to sleep with some semblance of serenity . . .

I moved into our place. I went out to find roles, immersed myself in acting classes and rehearsals, and came back every night, almost expecting to find her waiting for me in front of the fireplace, but instead I sat in the empty space and reread her letters. Every month, she sent me a check for her share of the rent, and to keep her warmth in the apartment, I always placed a fresh bouquet of flowers in the vase on top of the mantel, a reminder of her and the life we'd soon share.

Like clockwork, the next letter arrived. Wind Nymph! I'd

hustle up the stairs of the brownstone and shut the door to share this moment with her. What did she have for me this time?

Just to lie and stroke the worries from your forehead; to feel the length of my body next to yours; to feel the complete commitment of self unto another human being as or more important to you than you.

I hung onto every word of every letter, convinced in my naïveté that she was a deep intellectual, and responded with equally pretentious and sappy letters. But for all the written declarations of love and adoration, her actions spoke otherwise:

You see, I've got an absolutely fiendish sense of ambition, and though my intellect tells me it 'taint so important as other things, like immediate travel to you, I know it would insist on coming right along too and haunting me for the step I didn't climb, or the ones I lost.

I tried my best to be empathetic, while longing passionately for her. I had faith in Wind Nymph. The letters kept coming, but soon the rent checks that she sent to keep our place stopped. I would later learn the truth: While she was writing letters to me, she had developed a relationship with another actor. In the California breeze, my Wind Nymph was gone. I still have the letters.

Sometimes, Opportunity Knocking Sounds a Lot Like Bad Tennis

I remember the night-blooming jasmines, the honeysuckle of the desert, and the dust off desolate streets. When I first arrived in Phoenix, in February 1962, the city was nothing like the sprawling metropolis it is now. There were only a series of squat buildings and the main drag, Central Avenue. The big news in town was the arrival of a pair of neon golden arches that belonged to a new hamburger company called McDonald's, among the first locations in the country. The desert itself was breathtaking, the air dry and hot, and I can still see the clay, terra-cotta-colored dunes, and scrubby, cactus-covered flats.

I had been out West only in my mind. Until now, I knew only what had been shown to me by the fearless Roy Rogers, another hero of my youth, who taught me how to handle a vicious rattlesnake by removing his sidearm and blowing the serpent's head off. I was impressed.

In Phoenix, scanning the shrubs and dark corners for other

snakes, I reported for rehearsal at the Sombrero Playhouse, a nationally recognized theater financed by a cabal of Phoenix's wealthy philanthropists and a group who had agreed to fund an early run of *Natural Affection,* a play by William Inge. Inge was already an American legend for his plays *Come Back, Little Sheba* and *The Dark at the Top of the Stairs* and the film *Splendor in the Grass.* The director of the production was Harold Clurman, a heavy in New York theater circles, especially for his devotion to method acting and for forming the Group Theatre. His wife was Stella Adler, the famous acting coach, and after meeting Clurman in New York, I was truly lucky to get an audition and be cast in the play.

I couldn't believe I was working with so many talented and accomplished actors who had always been part of my fantasy life. Gil, my character, wasn't in many scenes in the play, so I worked double duty taking notes for Harold Clurman, who was all grown up by the fourth grade. He'd wear a full suit and wing-tip shoes to these rehearsals in the desert and masterfully handle the talent in the room. The male lead was Ralph Meeker, who had headlined a number of major films, including *Kiss Me Deadly,* and played a struggling car salesman. The female lead was Shelley Winters, already a big star. She'd come from the Midwest, changed her name from Shirley Schrift, and played a mother grappling emotionally with her son. I played Gil, a dope pusher, far down in the credits.

I spent hours watching and studying these wonderful actors, trying to learn all I could and absorb their tips and wisdom. I had the talent, I felt. I just needed experience and a break.

Shelley was a yenta. Oh, what a yenta Shelley could be. But

as an actor, she had tremendous emotional range. She could really turn on the tears.

To Harold Clurman, this wasn't a good thing. He wasn't buying it. Crying so hard—and so easily—felt fake, he said. It lacked emotion, didn't feel real.

"Shelley, it will be more impactful to play against crying," he told her. "Try and keep the tears in. Try to hold them back." He was brilliant. Seeing her on the stage struggling not to cry was so much more impactful. He said it to Winters, but I kept that note for myself: Less is more.

After the performances, we spilled out into Phoenix, walking through the doors of Durant's, the famous steakhouse known for its martinis and waiters in red tuxedo vests. The story goes that Jack Durant, the owner, had fled from Las Vegas after working as a pit boss for Bugsy Siegel at the Flamingo Hotel. After Bugsy was gunned down in Beverly Hills, Durant opened his doors here and came up with a midwestern marketing gimmick featuring forty-eight-ounce porterhouse steaks. Finish one, get your name on the wall.

It was lively on Central Avenue. The Playboy Club had opened a new location nearby, and to get inside the lair you needed a secret key that opened a secret elevator.

I never got a key. But I did have my adventures. Like the night I was propositioned for an orgy by an extra. She took me to a home outside of town where a massive gang bang was supposed to be going down.

I arrived and saw the crowd: retirees in leisure suits. I went back to my hotel immediately. I was chicken. This was too much. On the way into the hotel, I saw Rallie, a Phoenix socialite. I must have looked a little shaken up, so she did wonders to calm me down. What a memorable night we had, with the perfect ending: both of us on top of her mink coat on my hotel room's floor.

Shelley Winters was kind of a mess. She was never put together; she reminded me of my aunts who had come to visit us from the city carrying their plastic bags of dried fruit. The heels of her sneakers had all been run down, and she came off as half gypsy, half elderly bubbe. When we went out to dinner one night, someone accosted her for wearing her ratty gym sneakers.

"I'm a star. I can wear whatever the fuck I want to wear," she said, rather loudly.

Shelley was so grating and unpredictable that there were few in the cast who wanted to spend time with her. I didn't mind. I knew that to get anywhere in my career I would need the help of people like her. And, honestly? I became her friend, in spite of her brashness. When nobody else wanted to play tennis with her, I would.

I stepped in and hit an easy forehand her way.

"Oye!" she shrieked, shanking the ball into the fence.

I hit her another light backhand. Again came the cry, and I watched her chase after the ball, stumbling over her chubby legs.

"Aiiich," she shrieked again, hitting another ball into the air and off the court.

Once I was winded from chasing all the errant balls around, we stopped to relax. A bench was next to the court, and we sat there together. The run of Natural Affection was almost over, and soon the cast would be off to their next jobs. Except me, of course, who didn't have a next job. As usual.

Shelley was going back to Hollywood. She'd been picked to play the female lead in *Lolita*, based on the Nabokov novel. It was an incredible opportunity. Nabokov himself had written the screenplay, and Stanley Kubrick was chosen as the director. Shelley would be nominated for a Golden Globe for best actress.

"What are you going to do, Jono?" she asked me.

I didn't really have any plans, other than returning to New York and making the rounds again. Henry Fonda would later tell me that on the first day of any new job he would already be worried about what he'd do when it came to an end. Would he be out of work? Would the job he was on be the last one he ever did? That's just the reality of an actor's life. In the early days of my career, the average income of all Screen Actors Guild members was less than three thousand dollars per year. Being out of work brought with it the usual self-doubts, which always fluttered about in the corners of my mind. The ongoing rejection could take its toll on one's confidence and ability to go forward with that much-talked-about "best foot." It was a withering assault, and the constant battle was very personal, unlike that in almost any other field or endeavor. If a salesman's products are not accepted, it's not necessarily he who is getting rejected. I mean, it could be. But it could also be his products. But an actor's product is himself—his sensitivity, his talent, his looks, his very being. It takes a strong belief in oneself to continue after constant rejection and long periods of time out of work.

"No plans," I replied.

We sat quietly for a moment.

"You know," I offered cautiously, "I've never been to California." I hoped she'd pick it up from there.

She did. She liked me.

Hollywood was a good place for a young actor at my level, she said.

"But I'd need an agent, for sure, and I don't have one." Again, I hoped she'd pick up the hint.

Again, she did.

"Well, I'll introduce you to Herb Brenner."

Shelley may have been loud and outrageous, but she had a heart of gold, at her core a caring and sensitive person. She was influential in helping out a lot of actors. I'm glad I was one of them. I would later appear with her on Broadway in *The Night of the Iguana*, a play by Tennessee Williams. I know she had something to do with that too. It seemed like all my classes, studies, rejections, and roles were finally paying off. All that fetching of balls and trying to make Shelley look good on the court probably hadn't hurt either.

"He's a big agent," she remarked offhandedly.

Everyone knew the name Herb Brenner. He was a top agent at Music Corporation of America, or MCA, it was called, a powerhouse of an agency run by Lew Wasserman, a Hollywood legend who'd represented American household names like Bette Davis and Ronald Reagan.

All of a sudden, shrieking Shelley Winters had become a part of the fabric of my career. Even my own understanding of myself, perhaps as delusional as that was, had changed. Now I was an actor, with some prospects and a direct connection inside a premier Hollywood agency. I had a plan. What could stop me?

"I can make you a star, Jono, if you play your cards right," Shelley said.

She had given me a gift. And once I got back to the East Coast, I decided to take her up on her offer out west and seek my fortune with my new contact, even if it was only one. After all, it was Herb Brenner. But as I strategized my move to La-La Land, Shelley's parting words stuck with me: "If you play your cards right." What did Shelley mean? I'd soon find out.

Act II

I drove the '65 Ford diesel pickup toward the Dos Equis commercial audition, down the California coast, a place of extraordinary natural beauty. A vast place, one that offered a chance for extraordinary success and failure (more of the latter). I was reminded of how I loathed the status symbols of the industry and the fads of tony neighborhoods. Even staying in the Sycamore Canyon Campground, which was closer to Oxnard than to the studios of Century City, was a kind of badge of pride for me. I'd come to dislike the Hollywood elite, a shifting cabal of players who kept the power and budgets to themselves and chose directors and actors not on their talents but on the crude and unfair game of who was hot.

Of course, my animus toward the system was personal. I had fought so hard to break through to stardom over a forty-year career, and while I came to befriend some of the biggest stars, I never joined their ranks. My fate was different. For years, I tried to reconcile my close calls—there were many. So close to success, so often, only to have that dream disintegrate into disappointment. So much rejection, so much loss, takes its toll on a guy.

But the drive was also a reminder of what I had gained in a lifetime devoted to making it in Hollywood. As I drove down the Pacific Coast Highway, I was reminded of all my friends, acquaintances, lovers, even mobsters, cops, and mistresses, who had earned their rightful places in my memory. Hollywood was a land of illusion, for sure. But there had been so many moments—good and bad—that were so real.

It was hard not to reflect on how far I had come on drives like this. In fact, it was a drive like this that had brought me to Hollywood in the first place.

The Best Time to Go for Broke Is When You're Already Broke

Since I was living below the poverty line, I figured driving across the country to Los Angeles would be the most prudent and economical thing to do. Luckily, I already had a place to stay when I arrived: Walter Koenig, an actor friend best known for playing the role of Chekov in *Star Trek,* invited me to crash with him. I purchased a VW Bug, the most affordable car in America. And with its many thousands of already accrued miles, it was even more affordable.

At the time, so many students and young folks like myself were escaping the harsh realities of the moment—Vietnam, race riots, the rise of corporations—and driving aimlessly around the country to explore backwater towns, crash music festivals, and experiment on communes, but I was on a different mission: I wanted to connect with Herb Brenner, Shelley Winters's agent. I was anxious to meet him and get my movie career going.

I had planned the trip out west in the timeliest and most

affordable manner. By my calculations, I could make it across the country, all three thousand or so miles, in three full days. And by keeping my cheap little Bug moving all the time, driving through the night, I wouldn't have to pay for a hotel room. I soon realized I couldn't make the entire trip myself in that fashion, so I put in an ad at the Screen Actors Guild, looking for another actor to help me make the trip.

I prayed my companion would be a comely, busty redhead. Robert Porter, the fellow wayward actor who answered my ad, was certainly none of those things. He tossed his things into the back of the Beetle. So much for the bed, I thought.

Robert was a good enough guy who looked like James Dean and said very little as we filled up with gas and drove on out. I packed just the essentials: a toiletry kit, a few changes of clothes, and the only formal attire to my name: a navy blue suit and black Oxford shoes. I'd worn the suit on so many auditions. I could use it for casting calls in Hollywood too, I figured.

It didn't take long for Robert and me to get into a rhythm. We'd split the shifts in four- to five-hour segments. Him at the wheel, me asleep in the back amid our stuff, and vice versa. The first day, we passed the refinement plants and farms of New Jersey and crossed over into Pennsylvania, with its coal-mining plants and steel mills. Four hours on. Four hours asleep. When the weather was warm, we could spread out in the back, sticking a leg outside the window.

I didn't pay much attention to the country passing us by, so many urban centers converted to ghettos with the industrialization of the North, the migration of so many from the South. The news we listened to on the car radio painted a picture of a nation ripped apart at the seams, and we heard stories of riots and prison uprisings, killings, and the rumblings of a draft for the war in Vietnam. I did not want to fight. This was the wrong war. I was more at ease in the bohemian lifestyle.

In Oklahoma, I heard over the radio that the director who had seen me in the film *Act One* and was willing to give me Hollywood introductions had won an Emmy. It was a blast of positive news. The stars were aligning; my contemporaries were rising in status; naturally, I figured, they'd be able to help elevate me too. Emboldened by the positive response, we never stopped for long. Soon we crossed the Oklahoma border and then continued on down the Mother Road, America's Main Street, the historic Route 66. We passed through Amarillo on the way through the Texas panhandle, new motels sprouting up alongside the highway, their vacancy signs illuminating our passage and the long, lonely stretches in the deserts of New Mexico, hours of mesas and old mining towns, listening to the Beach Boys, dreaming of our new promised land.

I preferred driving the night shift, careening through the darkness under the brilliant stars of the desert. I loved looking up and getting lost in the emptiness of it all, the extreme quiet of night. Here, my mind was left to roam freely, imagining my heroes—Montgomery Clift, Sir Laurence Olivier, Albert Finney, Tom Courtenay, and Richard Attenborough, these extraordinary talents, masters of their craft, famous the world over. They too had followed their path to stardom and emerged wealthy and known. I could be up there too—if I played my cards right—whatever that meant.

The first winks of daylight were like the opening of an eye, the first blinks on earth, and reminders of those dawn fishing trips I had taken with my father. Now that I was on my own, these sunrises across the deserts were my own new memories. I enjoyed them even more because they were mine. Learning to embrace the silence of the dawn, listening to its secrets, and beginning to understand them was another sign that I had become my own man, and part of that realization was the unshakable reality that my destiny was my own. My life was actually happening. I had made a choice—to move west—and it was frightening. Had I made the right choice or the wrong choice? Were they both the same?

We barely made it into town. We battled some headwinds in the final push to Los Angeles and burned out the engine. I dropped off my travel companion—never saw him again—and limped the car to Koenig's apartment.

The apartment on Serrano Street was tiny, a cramped wing of a stucco cottage that was located between East Hollywood and Slumsville. He hadn't cleaned the place in honor of my arrival. In fact, I don't think he'd even wiped down the counters since he moved in years before. He was a heady intellectual, buried in scripts and books, and very involved with the Angels, a prestigious company of actors. He never bothered to clean the hair out of the sink or remove the fingernail clippings from the coffee table—or the kitchen table. He greeted me and then escorted me to my sleeping quarters: the couch. He'd picked it up from the curb, no doubt. And no, it hadn't been reupholstered. Or cleaned. I mummified myself in a sheet to keep the bugs away and slept with my shoes on for additional protection.

That's not to say I wasn't immensely grateful for his hospitality. We shared a lot of memories and a great friendship that spanned from the Neighborhood Playhouse in New York to LA. His role on *Star Trek* and his success were much deserved and truly could not have happened to a nicer guy.

For my first night, Koenig took me out. We went out on the Sunset Strip, the essence and pulsing heart of the Hollywood I had come to conquer, the portal of action. I had now opened the door and walked through its primary hub: the Whiskey a Go Go, or the Whiskey, for short. The Whiskey was the spot for music and hijinks in Los Angeles, a place where anyone could make it, they said, and nobody went home alone. The owner was a crooked cop with over-the-top taste.

The house band was the Doors, led by poetic wild man Jim Morrison. It was where the Byrds got big and everyone from Jimi Hendrix to Marilyn Monroe could be found amid the anonymous throngs.

I walked inside and was blown away. Suspended in two cages hanging from the ceiling were a pair of go-go dancers hovering over a cloud of marijuana smoke. The crowd was good-looking. The guys were muscular, the girls all tanned. Great dancing. Sexy dancing. Everybody was loaded and doing the monkey and the chicken. I knew it. I had made it. As Woody Allen famously said, "Eighty percent of success is showing up." And I had. Now all I needed to do was focus on the other twenty percent, whatever that was.

I was to find out it was a lot harder than driving across the country in a clown car.

If at First You Don't Succeed,
Get Used to It

I looked up Herb Brenner to make an appointment. I called the office and waited for this gatekeeper of fame to call me back.

"Mr. Brenner is not in. Who may I say is calling?" the secretary said.

I dropped Shelley Winters's name, left my number, and went out to explore Los Angeles. The city, I found, was a fairy tale of sensuality. I loved the way the palm trees towered over me and I could hear the clatter of their fronds, smell the warm odor of orange blossoms, and hear the splatter of fountains. And the women, so beautiful, walking around in their flat Capezio shoes.

The sunny days passed and started to blend into one another. A week passed. What had happened to Herb Brenner? Was he ever going to call me back? I tried the office again, left another message. Maybe he was on vacation? Should I swing by? The more I thought about it, the more I couldn't believe the nerve of this guy. Shelley Winters was a big star. How about some attention, Herb?

Eventually, he called. I jumped into my blue suit and Oxfords and went to meet him at his office.

"Welcome to Hollywood," he said.

"Thanks," I said.

"What's with the suit? Actors don't wear suits on the West Coast. They wear T-shirts."

"Well, this is my first week here."

"I have bad news," he said.

"Oh?"

"I'm afraid I can't help you."

"Huh?"

"We can't take you on."

"You haven't seen me act yet. Shelley Winters said—"

"Yeah, I know what Shelley said, but Shelley is female. And she's Shelley Winters. I have too many young male clients who look just like you. They come first."

I walked out of the office deflated, torn. Too many clients? Fuck Herb Brenner. What was I going to do? I was broke. I had only a few dollars, a dirty couch to live on, and a Volkswagen Bug with a blown engine. I had to find a job. And an agent. Being turned down by the famous Mr. Brenner was heartbreaking. I felt like giving up, but the ongoing rejection was instead an inspiration for me to stay in the fray. My father told me, when I was a kid: "A Goldsmith never gives up." Over the years to come, Los Angeles was going to test that determination.

Never Make It Final

Without an agent, I had to rely on the few connections I did have. I called on William Inge, the playwright from *Natural Affection,* the play we put on at the Sombrero in Phoenix. We'd traded letters, and soon after I arrived in Los Angeles, Inge invited me to his home.

"I'm having a painting party," he told me, and so I set off into the Hollywood Hills to find his upscale cottage, which was tucked in on one of the streets named for birds—Oriole or Robin. I found the home, went inside, and stepped onto a drop cloth, one of many covering the home's floors. The open windows looked out over the city. Wow, I thought: This really is Los Angeles. Looking around at the guests Inge had assembled, I noticed they all had some things in common: All were young guys, all good-looking, and all fluttering about with brushes and rollers.

Wait a second.

Not that I had any problem with gay guys, of course. I was from the theater scene in New York, a self-styled bohemian. Not my cup of tea, but to each his own.

Then Inge appeared, welcoming me to his home. He was giggly.

"Would you like to take a shower?" he asked me.

"Oh, c'mon, Bill. Take one of these guys," I said, pointing to the collection of young bucks he'd assembled.

"It's just a shower," he said. "I'll do your back."

I demurred, but in a flattering, self-deprecating, and joking way. We became close friends. Inge was sick. Though he was a recovering alcoholic of some years, he was still a depressive. He spent hours talking to me, revealing these deep thoughts. Once, I told him, "I lay awake at night for hours thinking, How am I going to get there?"

Inge had heard it all before.

"I lay awake at night for hours too, thinking, How am I going to stay there?" he told me.

Inge was troubled.

"I'm probably going to kill myself," he told me one day.

"Well, I hope that you don't," I said.

"No, I'm going to kill myself," Inge said.

"The sun comes up, the day changes," I said, reminding him of the fleeting nature of emotions. The rationale was not good enough. Soon after our last talk, I received news that Inge had gone out to his garage in that same charming cottage, started his car's engine, filled the chamber with carbon monoxide, and killed himself just like he'd told me he would.

"Death makes us all innocent," Inge had written, "and

weaves all our private hurts and griefs and wrongs into the fabric of time, and makes them a part of eternity."

Inge's death preyed on me. At night, I thought my own dark thoughts, which accompanied each fresh rejection and crept often into my mind. I wondered, having these thoughts that plagued me too: Could I do it? Could I go through with it like Inge, given the pain I sometimes felt? Sure, I could make everyone laugh, but in the process, hearing all the laughter, I wondered: Don't they get it? I'm in a lot of pain here. How can they not see that? What's the matter with them?

At daybreak, relief would set in. The air would fill with light and deliver a new morning, a new chance to find a role. Several months had passed and I knew success for me would never be about talent, luck, or connections. My path would have to be about endurance. As Vernon Scott, a critic friend from the *Hollywood Reporter*, once told me after working out in a gym, "You have to outlast the bastards."

Even the Lowliest Job
Can Lead to Another Job

I f I was going to outlast the bastards, I'd need to last. I needed a job to sustain me as I pursued my acting career. For a lead, I scanned the Rolodex in my mind for the name of a friend, an acquaintance, even a stranger I had met only once who might live in Los Angeles and could help. I remembered Jack Brown, whom I had appeared with in a few scenes back in New York. I looked him up and told him I was looking for work, and he recommended I visit the main office of a construction company he knew. They were always hiring. The pay was terrible, he warned, but the work was immediate. No questions asked.

Jack was right. I went to the office and was offered a job on the spot: garbageman. Just perfect. My duties were simple: arrive on a construction site with a truck, load it with industrial waste, and drive it out to the dump. The hours ranged from dawn until late. The pay was a pittance: three dollars an hour. I graciously accepted, but the labor was brutal. I'd arrived in Los

Angeles in the dead of summer, and by midmorning the temperatures had reached ninety degrees and climbing. My garbage truck had no air-conditioning, of course, and I'd drive across the valley to sites in Calabasas to pick up waste—ratty insulation or industrial scraps of old pipes, tar paper, and general debris, all dusted over with a demi-glace of rat shit—then drag it all out to the dump. Even in those days the traffic was relentless, and to catch a break I'd lie in the shade of a palm tree in a park, wondering how I'd messed up by moving west. My life had become a wreck, and I was on the precipice, unclear if I had the personal fortitude to work my way back.

Looking for a better job, I stopped off at the unemployment office. It was the happening place. The steadiest form of income for actors in the union, of which I was a member, was the unemployment checks we could claim between jobs. The office was at the intersection of Santa Monica Boulevard and Las Palmas in Hollywood, and we all hung out there. It was a networking event and social mixer rolled into one, with the added bonus of free money. You'd see the extras in their rags and the stars with their chauffeurs and big cars parked out front. I never saw it, but I heard my friend Shelley Winters showed up occasionally with her driver in a limo and picked up her unemployment check wearing a mink coat.

We developed a routine. After we got our checks, we'd head down the street to the Formosa Cafe for Chinese food. The Formosa was a nexus of Hollywood's misfits: mobsters, screenwriters, boxers. The menu was Cantonese, but the owner was Jimmy Bernstein. He'd been in the fight game so long that the country's most famous boxers—legends like Jack Dempsey and

Joe Louis—would swing by, along with executives from Goldwyn Studios across the street. The place was made from an old trolley car, with deep, red leather booths and dim lighting. We sat there for hours, wondering who might come in. Elvis Presley was such a regular at the Formosa, we heard, he once gave a waitress there a Cadillac as a tip.

I hadn't gotten an acting job in so long that the unemployment checks ran out, and I had to find another job. I was tired of hauling garbage, so the unemployment office assigned me a caseworker.

"So, what kind of work are you looking for?" she asked me.

"Anything," I told her.

"Are you handy? You do carpentry, plumbing, painting, that kind of thing?"

"Of course," I said, lying through my teeth. I couldn't even fix a toilet.

"Would you mop floors?" she asked.

"Anything," I said, sighing.

"I might have something for a young man of your talents," she said, and instructed me to purchase my own mop and pail and to report for work the next day. She didn't tell me what I'd be doing with the mop and pail but handed me a slip of paper with an address on Roxbury Drive in Beverly Hills. This didn't sound promising, but that address would change the course of my career.

Before it became known as a home for Hollywood's elite, Beverly Hills was a lima bean farm. At the turn of the century, a developer purchased all the farms there, hoping to dig for oil. The testing proved the land was dry, so the developer needed another way to turn those old lima bean farms into lucrative parcels. So he built the Beverly Hills Hotel, a destination resort for actors and others en route to Los Angeles. The first movie stars stayed there and settled, building their mansions near the hotel, where the beans once grew. The first to go up was Pickfair, the massive twenty-five-room Tudor-style estate owned by Mary Pickford and Douglas Fairbanks, with horse stables, a tennis court, a swimming pool, and frescoes painted on the ceiling.

The scions of early film—Charlie Chaplin, Buster Keaton, Will Rogers—all built their estates near Pickfair, and the neighborhood when I arrived still had its own star map. Elvis Presley lived on Peruvia Way. Kirk Douglas was on North Canon. Doris Day, on North Crescent. James Stewart was on Roxbury, where I was headed, only a few blocks away.

I was walking through Beverly Hills with my new mop and pail when I passed by Jergens, then a famous fruit and vegetable stand. The colors of the fabulous fruit outside triggered my salivary glands. I was still always hungry. I was saving every dollar, so after surveying the strawberries, watermelons, and mangoes, I made a frugal choice: a banana. Did I pay for it? Did I steal it? Does it matter? In those days, a piece of stolen fruit wasn't the end of the world. Who'd miss a banana?

The temperatures were rising, and I found a spot of shade. I rested the mop against the tree, flipped over my new pail, and sat down. My shirt was soaked with sweat and I removed it to air it out. I had just started to eat when I heard a voice.

"Hey, come here."

I turned. A Beverly Hills police officer was staring at me.

"Me?" I mumbled, mouth full of banana.

"Yeah, you. What are you doing?"

"Eating my breakfast, Officer." I swallowed. "And going to work."

He asked me for identification. I didn't have any. Now I had to convince him I was not an illegal border worker from El Salvador with my mop and pail but instead an aspiring actor from New York. This copper had no sense of humor.

"You don't walk around Beverly Hills like that," he said, pointing at my shirt and demanding I put it back on. I obediently obliged. I'd come to Los Angeles wanting to live in Beverly Hills, not get arrested there for eating a banana topless.

He was right, though. You didn't walk around Beverly Hills like that. In fact, no one walked around Beverly Hills at all, or anywhere else in Los Angeles. Except me.

I finally made my way to Roxbury Drive. The palm trees here were taller and the houses bigger, it seemed. The lawns were all set back, and Mexican gardeners tended to the hedges as luxury cars sparkled in the driveways. I walked up the path, and Rita Rubins opened the door to greet me. She was wearing a muumuu. A cigarette dangled from her lip. She was a buxom blonde, a little overweight. A lovely woman: warm and voluptuous.

She gave me a tour, and as we walked through her immaculate home, she told me about her past. She had come to Los Angeles and married Paul Whitcomb, a major director. He'd once been under contract at Columbia Pictures and made several features, all so boring and unmemorable I can't name a single one. I do, however, recall seeing him pass through the house in his jodhpurs and monocle, fancying himself a Yiddish version of Erich von Stroheim. Despite his arrogance, this obnoxious director had lived in town for more than twenty years and was a great connection for me to develop. I hoped he could find me work on sets and make my career.

I soon learned that Rita was lonely, alienated from her pretentious husband. He was never around, she complained. Just left her behind, she said, as we proceeded to go over my first assignment: mopping floors. She also asked if I could build a small shed. "Of course," I confidently replied. I went to the store, got all the parts and supplies, and proceeded to create a disaster. I had my doubts it would last the season, and when the first fall breeze blew, it fell down. I was totally inept.

My next project was painting the bedroom for Herman, their son, who was mentally challenged. I screwed it up so many times she let me come up with the splatter-paint design for the floor, à la Jackson Pollock, to cover up all the messes. I couldn't do any of the jobs right. Rita didn't complain. She was attracted to me and desperate for the affection her husband never gave her.

We developed a friendly routine. I'd arrive each morning, and she'd cook me the same breakfast: scrambled eggs and cottage cheese. Sitting across from me, ubiquitous cigarette dangling from her lip, she'd be the first of many married women to reveal they were starved for passion. The more we talked, the more the tension between Rita and me escalated. And one day, we ended up on the floor of the maid's bathroom. In truth, it was kind of glorious.

I felt a little guilty about the indulgence. After all, I hadn't come to Hollywood to satisfy the desires of married women. I wanted to be an actor, and if Rita's powerful husband discovered our dalliances, I'd never have a chance with him. I might not just lose a good connection; I could be blackballed among Holly-wood's insular hive.

Not that I had a shot with Otto von Stroheim, anyway. He was a prick, I'd quickly learn. Egotistical, slightly maniacal. Rita would invite me to all these parties he threw at the house for their actor friends, and he'd have all these starlets there and not pay any attention to Rita. That was now my job.

Over breakfast one morning, she startled me.

"You know, you're a jerk," she said.

"Why do you say that, Rita?"

"You're giving it away."

I didn't know what she meant at first.

"I'm going to fix you up with somebody who's really going to take good care of you."

"I'm not a fucking gigolo," I said.

She pointed her finger at me.

"Be smart," she said. "You're a good-looking kid. Use your assets. Don't be a schmuck."

Then she told me about Beth.

"She's a little older," she said.

"How old?"

"Late fifties," Rita said.

I felt queasy. My mother was in her late fifties.

"She's put together," Rita said.

"What does that mean?"

"She plays three-wall handball. What can I tell you?"

"I don't know, Rita," I said, not convinced. "What can you tell me?"

"Her husband owns a casino in Las Vegas," she said.

Great. Another married woman with a powerful husband. Only this time, instead of getting tarnished among a small group of film executives, I'd wind up in a grave near the Hoover Dam. Back then, all of Las Vegas's hotels and casinos were run by the mob.

"He doesn't bother with her at all," Rita said, going on about Beth's mobbed-up husband. "They don't have a marriage. It's just in name only."

I wasn't convinced.

"Look, putz, she took her hairdresser to Paris and bought him a wardrobe, and he's a fagelah! You could really score!"

At the breakfast table, my scrambled eggs and cottage cheese were getting cold.

"Look at you," she said. "You need some clothes. You need a shirt and tie."

I tried to fight her. Really, I did. But I am not proud to admit I eventually succumbed to Rita's urging and went along with her plan. Instead of working to try to rebuild the shed that morning, I got into Rita's car and she drove me to Saks. We went up to the men's section, and I tried on a crisp white shirt, found a tie I liked, and took them both home. I hadn't purchased new clothes in years and was touched that Rita would make the gesture. We were good friends. So good, we never made it back to the maid's bathroom.

"This is very nice of you," I said appreciatively.

"Just play your cards right and she'll treat you well," she said. "You deserve it."

Play your cards right. Aha. Now I was getting to know what that phrase meant.

"You'll be meeting her at the Beverly Wilshire Hotel. You know where that is?"

I had frequently passed the Beverly Wilshire Hotel when I was hauling garbage. It was and still is frequented by stars and movers in all aspects of show business. There was a coffee shop on the street level called the Pink Turtle. I would see the most beautiful array of starlets going into the lobby, as well as the café. From my vantage point in the truck, there seemed to be an unusual amount of these lovelies convening there, even in a town known for beautiful women. They were young, tanned, and dressed to kill, be it nine in the morning, when I started my route, or later in the day, when I was returning. I had to investigate.

I began to frequent the Pink Turtle. Their scrambled eggs were delicious (although not as good as Rita's) and not outrageously priced. I soon uncovered the reason for the marvelous and endless parade of women, and it would prove a major boost to my social life: Warren Beatty. He lived in the penthouse of the hotel, and I found an ingenious way to break the ice.

"Hi! Are you waiting to see Warren?" I would inquire. Thinking I was an aide-de-camp and a conduit to the legendary lothario, they would light up and be extremely receptive to dialogue.

"Well, Warren's tied up at the moment. But he asked me to buy you a drink." Most were eager to comply—at least now they were on his radar. The Wilshire bar was a bit upscale for my garbageman's salary, so I would whisk them down the street to a Chinese restaurant that had a great—and reasonable—happy hour.

So, yes, Rita. I knew where the Beverly Wilshire Hotel was.

"Okay, brief me: How old is she again?" I asked.

"Early sixties," Rita said.

"Early sixties? I thought you said fifties!"

I was nervous, embarrassed, a bit ashamed, but curious to see where this adventure was going and too desperate to turn it down.

Steal Nothing but Hearts

I walked into the lobby of the Beverly Wilshire Hotel and called up to her room on the house phone. "Hello, Beth, this is Jonathan," I said, feeling the pools of sweat gather in my socks. Could I really spend an evening with a woman in her early sixties? And the wife of a casino mogul, perhaps a gangster with mob ties? I thought about escaping, running back through the lobby of the hotel, with its marble columns and mahogany-and-walnut-paneled walls, and past the Oak Room, the famous bar and restaurant and a Hollywood bastion, the place where I really wanted to go.

"Hello, dear," Beth said, and the aging quiver in her voice put me into a state of mild shock. Beth was too old to be in her early sixties. She must have been in her midseventies.

"Come on up, dear," she croaked.

I walked into the elevator, my new shirt sopping with sweat. How could I do this? What had I become? Would Rita be upset?

How could I let her down after she'd been so nice and cooked me all those eggs with cottage cheese? Maybe I could cut the evening short, feigning a migraine.

The elevator door opened. She was waiting to meet me, sticking her leg out of the doorframe—a leg that reminded me of the atrophied chicken drumstick my uncle once left in the countertop oven for far too long.

I inched closer to the door and could see more of Beth now. She was closer to eighty and had a twinkle in her one good eye. She was wearing an expensive blue dress, and her bone-gray hair was pulled back in a chignon.

"Come on in, dear," she warbled, extending her hand, the bony fingers coming my way like a claw. I recoiled, and then I saw it. On one of her talons was the largest diamond I had ever seen. That rock must have been worth millions. Her husband probably didn't just own a casino. He could have been a capo too.

"Let's have a drink, dear," she chortled, ushering me to the couch and wriggling toward me, pulling up her blue gown and revealing her knobby knees. Beth wasn't as old as my mother. She was as old as my grandmother. She leaned in closer and I panicked and stood up.

"Perhaps we could get something to eat," I said, thinking that a retreat to a restaurant would allow me the chance to slip away from this old crone. To this day, I feel guilty talking ill of people, but there is no other way to describe her.

"Splendid idea," she said. "Why don't we order room service, dear, and get to know each other?"

Room service?! Damn it, Beth knew the drill. How to escape?

"You know, Beth, I've never been in the Oak Room," I said,

referring to the famous restaurant downstairs. I went on about how all the stars went there and how I'd always wanted to go.

"All right, dearie," she said, and she creaked slowly and laboriously to her feet. We walked out of the apartment, a mink coat draped over her skeletal frame. Down toward the elevator, she grabbed onto my elbow.

The beginnings of an anxiety attack swept over me. What if anyone saw me? What would they think? It looked as though I was dating my grandmother. Surely, someone in the hotel would tip off Mr. Mogul, her almost certainly mobbed-up husband. Had Rita said he was from Chicago? I thought about the added pain. How low had I fallen?

The Oak Room was as I'd expected. The light was low, the wood dark and rich, the waiters in white coats. In the banquettes around us, I spotted a mix of Hollywood elite sipping martinis, and around the room, a covered silver-domed wagon passed with hors d'oeuvres.

I ordered a spread of appetizers, the smoked salmon with dill sauce and Italian salami—none of which I was able to enjoy despite being famished. Under the table, I felt Beth's knees searching to connect with my own. To slow her advances, I looked down at the table and commented on her diamond ring.

"Oh yes," she said, admiring her stone. "This is bigger than Liz Taylor's diamond."

I wish I'd never heard her say that. My mind started spinning. Liz Taylor's diamond was a monster of a stone, more than thirty-three carats, and worth millions. After driving a garbage truck and hauling insulation for three dollars an hour, a fortune like that was powerfully seductive. One rock alone could purchase a home in Los Angeles, a home back east, a nice car. I could pursue acting, perhaps even consider directing or writing like Jimmy Boanes, a friend who'd made a career writing Westerns and television shows. Nobody had heard from Jimmy, though—not after he went for a weekend in Lake Tahoe, fixed a game of keno for twenty-five thousand dollars, and then fled to Borneo, where he was probably living like a king. Borneo wasn't too bad a place, I figured, having dark thoughts. Perhaps if I could get away with Beth's monster diamond, I could sell the stone for a fortune and meet up with Jimmy. Or find my own paradise.

I hated myself for these thoughts ricocheting around in my mind. I quickly and silently cut a deal with God Almighty. Just this once, God, please, and I'll never do anything like this again. I'll send half—no, a quarter; that's still a lot—of the proceeds to charity: the Red Cross, St. Jude, etc. And of course, I'll never have to worry about a paycheck for years. I could act full-time. That's a good deal, right?

The restaurant was clearing out, the waiters closing up. I couldn't stall any longer.

"Let's go upstairs," Beth said, placing her hands on top of mine.

I started to cough and grabbed my throat as if it were having a spasm.

"You know, Beth, I have acute pharyngitis, right here," I said, having learned long ago that if you're going to lie, be specific. "I need to walk; I need the night air."

I stood up from the table and put on my trench coat. It had been raining outside.

"Okay, dearie," she told me, ogling me hungrily with her one good eye. "We'll walk first and then we'll go upstairs."

"That's fine, Beth," I said, helping her with her mink, blinded by the shine of that fucking diamond.

Outside the hotel, the night was cool and damp. A light mist swept over us as we walked down Wilshire, the path of the stars. The traffic passed us as we turned on the sidewalk, listening to the sound of tires splashing in the wet street. I put my hands inside my raincoat to keep them warm and wondered: How am I going to get out of this? What will Rita say? Then it hit me again: How much is Beth's diamond really worth? Could I get away with it? I felt ashamed of myself. After all, my great-grandfather had founded a yeshiva.

My musings on morality and riches were disturbed by a sensation inside my raincoat pocket. It was Beth. The old girl was persistent and had burrowed her clawlike hand into my trench coat. She was holding on to me, nestling her fingers between my own, and as she did so I felt that damn seductive ring. I could feel the cool, spiky gold crown holding up the jewel, just another trophy rock for Beth, but a stone that could elevate me from poverty and finance the rest of my life.

I decided to go for broke. I actively began to manipulate her hand, trying to coax the ring from her finger inside my jacket pocket, a gesture she mistook for an amorous advance. She was caressing my fingers, desperate for tenderness, and I was caressing her fingers too, desperate to pry the band of the ring loose from her bony finger. I felt the diamond and pushed it just so, trying to ease it off her finger and into my coat pocket.

The stone wouldn't budge.

I tried harder and she started massaging my hand even faster, digging deeper into my pocket, continuing to confuse my efforts for advances of ardor. Then her hand and ring were out of mine, as she continued through my pocket and proceeded to grab my balls.

I panicked. I saw the light of a taxicab and jumped out into the street, the dazzling luminescence of traffic lights and high beams shining on the wet pavement.

"I've got to go," I said, delivering an apologetic salute and disappearing inside a cab. I cursed my poor luck, but I was fortunate. If it weren't for Beth's arthritic knuckle, I'd probably still be in prison. I had the chance to play my cards right, but the hand I was dealt turned out to be more of a claw.

I'd been in Los Angeles for only a few months. Already I was losing my grip. My morals were slipping. I had to change. I had turned into the kind of young man even I could not respect.

When Life Puts You Low, Start Climbing

I decided to put the reins on my careers as a gigolo and jewel thief. I was in need of fresh air and a touch of salvation. While I was driving my garbage truck for the construction company, milling around the office one afternoon, I met Larry McGregor. He was a marine, about my age, and working for extra pay while on furlough from Vietnam. We became friends. Stuck in the noisy, smog-choked city, we always talked about taking a trip into the High Sierra to get some perspective, and one of the more popular hikes within driving range was Mount Whitney, the highest peak in the continental United States. Only the peaks of Denali (formerly Mount McKinley) and others in the Alaskan and Yukon ranges stood taller. The dangers of Mount Whitney were well-known. Even though it was common for novice hikers to put in for permits to make the climb, the jagged passes, thin air, and rapidly changing weather could turn Whitney into a death trap.

Mount Whitney has a legend too. It is said that the Paiute tribe, the Native Americans who claimed the borders of Nevada and the High Sierra Nevada mountain ranges as their home-land, believed the mountain harbored the spirit of an old man. Too-man-i-goo-yah, they called him, which translates to "old wise one." Long before mountaineers and alpine conservation-ists discovered it, the Paiute considered the mountain spirit a ruling leader, a supreme force who looked down from the craggy, majestic heights and passed judgment on those who mis-behaved and did not live up to the tribe's code of ethics.

My recent dalliances with married women and brushes with grand theft were probably pretty significant evidence that I had not been living up to the tribe's code of ethics—or any standard of ethics at all. But how bad could Too-man-i-goo-yah's judgment really be?

I was tempted to make the climb alone, inspired by the physical challenge, but when I mentioned it to Larry at the con-struction company, he wanted to come along. We agreed to make the hike together. We put in for a permit and were accepted. I started to train. I bought a Kelty pack, the type that had been used on one of the first ascents to the peak of Mount Everest. Kelty was rapidly becoming the choice of knowledgeable backpackers. They had a special frame that would take the strain off the lower back. Larry was stronger than I was, and to pull my own weight on the hike I had to bulk up. I then created my own alpine hiking regi-men. I'd stuff my Kelty with books and cans and other stuff to make it as heavy as possible, then walk around in my short sleeves in sunny Southern California, imagining the chilly winds we'd soon encounter once we arrived on the mountain.

Over the following months, Larry and I met often to plan the hike. We went over the topographical maps. I'd trace our routes as Larry followed along through his thick glasses. Without them, he could barely see.

"How blind are you?" I joked.

"Let's put it this way," he said. "Without them I could get lost in my own bathroom."

We did the research. Whitney commanded respect. The mountain was plagued by lightning. When the first official climb was completed in 1904, one of the first three hikers was struck by lightning on the mountain's flat plateau, which towered high over California and Nevada. He perished. The hike itself was also potentially perilous. As the climb became more popular, so many hikers applied for permits that the parks department had to limit the number of camping permits to maintain and protect the area. Without permission to spend the night, many tried to speed up the process and make the eleven-mile hike to the summit in only a day. Rising before dawn, they'd race up the trail, only to succumb to altitude sickness and freezing weather. Without packing proper clothes or supplies, these hikers could find themselves dizzy and disoriented. Once darkness crept in, if the moon was hidden or bad weather set in, it was easy to lose one's way on the narrow trail. Hikers would stumble around the trail and lose their way on the mountain's edges. The drops were steep, and hikers simply fell off. A misstep could cause a catastrophic plunge. Fallen hikers' bodies weren't found until the mountain lupine were in bloom for the six weeks spring visited the area. Each year, the local newspapers would report yet another hiker who'd gone missing. In total, more than three hundred hikers had entered the Whitney Portal to climb Mount Whitney and never came back alive. Hopefully, we wouldn't be among them.

Ａt was fall when we left, the kind of day in late September that brings a deeper chill when the sun starts to descend in the sky earlier, and we made our way to Lone Pine, the closest town to Whitney Portal and an outpost on the way to Death Valley. We signed in at the rangers' station, leaving our names and our time of entry—this way, the rangers knew who was out there in case they needed to send any search teams—and started the hike to Mirror Lake, which, at almost eleven thousand feet, many used as a base camp to acclimatize. Larry and I considered attempting the hike in a day, like more ambitious and experienced hikers, but decided we weren't foolish enough to attempt it all in one shot. The darkness one hiked through to complete the ascent at such speed was a danger, but so was the risk of altitude sickness. I'd had it before, fishing nearby in the High Sierra at only half the altitude of Mount Whitney. The constant nausea, strange fatigue, and difficulty breathing are awful. The vomiting is never fun either.

We started early enough, but we were slow. Years earlier, I had injured my toe. I was eighteen, working at the Herald Tribune Fresh Air Camp, whose aim was to provide participation in outdoor and aquatic activities for all kids, both able and disabled. I was carrying a child suffering epileptic seizures across a railroad track when I jammed my toe on a tie. It would never be the same. Now, here in Whitney Portal, the pain was increasing with each step. When we arrived at Mirror Lake, we set up camp. I was looking forward to a good night's sleep and getting rid of the damn headache I'd had since morning, an early indicator of possible altitude sickness. The moonlight was bright, illuminating the mountains around us. I took a sleeping pill to help ensure slumber and drifted off. We would need our energy for the summit the following day.

In the morning, we lightened our loads to just day packs, caching our big packs with the tent and clothing, except what we needed for the climb to the summit. We took our down jackets, water, extra socks, and a tiny medical kit with extra bandages for the blisters that would more than likely come, particularly on the descent. We started early enough, hoping to return to base camp, if not all the way out to the portal, in twilight. My foot was not getting any better. In fact, the pain was increasing. We moved so slowly that Larry and I were the last ones on the mountain before sunset. The last mile, with its ninety or so switchbacks, was exhausting. Three steps, one breath. As we finally neared the summit, we saw something. Something odd. It was another hiker, coming down the path, an old Speed Graphic camera and tripod over his shoulder. Why was he so late?

Obviously, he wasn't an experienced backpacker—folks have been known to limit the size of the toilet paper roll they carry, take only the smallest toothbrush and toothpaste. Some would even cut the handle off the toothbrush. They'd carry only dehydrated food. This guy had a heavy camera and tripod.

We said hello. His name was Bobby Richards. He was an amateur photographer, a retiree from Tucson, Arizona, he said. He was there with his wife, and Bobby thought he'd hike up to the summit to take a few pictures.

I couldn't believe what he was wearing: thin sneakers instead of boots, a T-shirt instead of a sweater, and a jean jacket instead of a parka. He certainly wasn't dressed for this kind of climb. What was he thinking? I thought.

The sun was falling, bringing a deeper chill. Bobby Richards disappeared down the trail, and Larry and I kept pushing on, needing to reach the summit and make our way back down the trail before dark, at least to Mirror Lake.

Finally, we were there. The view of majestic peaks turning purple in the twilight was awe-inspiring. From here, the highest point in the lower forty-eight states, we could see the lowest point—Death Valley—more than a hundred miles in the distance. I produced a flask of brandy, brought along to make a toast on the summit.

"My good man," I said, passing him the flask, "we made it!"

There was little time to celebrate, though. The sun was falling and it was turning cold. Just a few photos in the long shadows surrounding us, then we turned back down the trail, picking up our pace, my foot throbbing. I was very much looking forward to picking up our gear and flashlights and proceeding out to the portal, where my truck awaited, promising a long sleep in the back of the camper. Making our way down the switchbacks, we had to be careful—we were tired and going a little too fast. In the poor light with the shadows deep, it was easy to slip. Then I felt a tickle on my face.

Snow.

Setting up camp at Mirror Lake had been wise. We arrived there and realized we'd have to spend the night on the mountain, but we had shelter and supplies. Our tube tent was there, along with our food and water. I checked out my swollen toe. I massaged it to ease the pain. We enjoyed a drink, the last of the brandy. Then we laughed together in the dark and the gathering snowstorm.

"My hands are numb," Larry said, chuckling.

"How about we celebrate tomorrow in Malibu?" I laughed. "We can stop off and take a swim."

We settled in for some well-deserved rest. But I couldn't rest. Something was bothering me. Bobby. Our photographer friend. The one in sneakers and a jean jacket.

He was still out there.

I instinctively began to put my socks back on.

"We have a problem," I said.

"Whaddya mean?" Larry said, still dreaming of Malibu.

"The guy with his camera is still out there," I said.

Bobby Richards was out there, navigating the snow and darkness in his sneakers and T-shirt. Unlike us, he had not set up camp. It was getting cold, the wind picking up, and it looked like a whiteout was descending on us. It was.

"If he can't make it down, he'll freeze," Larry said.

Having little choice, we packed up everything quickly and set out back into the darkness. The storm's intensity continued to pick up, the wind howling and the snow thickening. Flashlights in hand, we headed down cautiously. After a few moments I heard Larry cursing behind me.

"Everything okay?" I hollered.

"No."

"What?"

"I lost my fucking glasses," he said. "The wind just blew them away." We began feeling around the trail in the dark for the frames of his glasses, careful not to crush the lenses with our boots. But the recovery of Larry's glasses was a hopeless cause, and eventually we turned our attention to the recovery of Mr. Richards. We moved farther down the trail. Larry began to stumble and fall. He was a powerful, strong man, but without his thick glasses he was helpless. He was descending a precipitous trail not only in a snowstorm but also with blurred vision. Given our increasingly imperiled situation, I thought of those statistics and stories of Whitney hikers who simply fell off the mountain. Would Larry become one of them? Would I follow? And where the hell was Bobby Richards and his damn camera?

Knowing we could easily get three feet of snow up there, we tried to move fast. To steady himself, Larry put his hand on my shoulder. Together, we eased down the trail, one step at a time, as the snow picked up. Without crampons we were constantly slipping. Larry might as well have been blind, and now I could barely see; one flashlight had been lost and the other was rapidly losing power. We were sliding on the rocks and feeling around in the darkness, knowing the sheer drop-offs were one false move away. The mountain felt alive.

"We gotta get off this mountain," I said to Larry as he held on to my shoulder, careful not to slip on the snowy trail.

"What about the hiker?"

"Maybe we'll stumble on the guy," I said, testing the snowy trail with my feet and inching us down, struggling forward into the dark oblivion. Then we heard a noise. A moan.

Bobby Richards, the foolish day-tripper, was huddled between a pair of rocks, moaning into the wind. I could tell he was dehydrated and had to be damn near frozen. We got him to his feet, rubbing his arms and smacking his legs to get the blood flowing. I rifled through my pack and found a pair of socks, which I placed on his hands as makeshift mittens. I had a poncho, and we placed that on him, shielding him slightly from the wind and the snow.

He was in bad shape. We had to get him down immediately, and ourselves with him. Together, we formed a chain. We draped Bobby's arms over my neck so I could hold his socked hands and block some of the wind that was pummeling us all. Larry was behind Bobby to keep him moving and held on to the poncho to steady himself without his glasses.

We didn't get far. We were all exhausted, and it was hard to gain our footing. Leading, I struggled to stay on the trail. The slipping and sliding increased, and I found myself taking a few steps off the trail to find better footing, not knowing where my steps would lead us. Then the remaining flashlight went out.

"We'll go off this fucking mountain if we keep going," I yelled back into the wind.

New plan: Instead of descending through the storm, we'd try to make camp. Trying to find my footing, I stumbled into a shallow crevice big enough to hold the three of us. We'd try to spend the night on the mountain and wait for the light of dawn and hopefully sun and warmth to rescue us. We had a pair of down sleeping bags. Bobby Richards was delirious. We laid him down on the ground, put him inside my mummy bag, and poured some of the last drops of our water into his mouth. He either fell asleep or lapsed into a coma instantly. Worried about him, I wrapped him in the light cord from our tube tent, tying the other end around my arm. Larry was a big guy, so he and I could fit only halfway into the other mummy bag, but we had on our down jackets, and if they didn't get wet they would keep us warm.

We just huddled there together, praying for the snow to stop and the sun to come up in the morning. But time never moves slower than when the elements—pain, cold, hunger—strike. The warm sands of Malibu seemed millions of miles away. I thought about the strange delivery of Bobby Richards and my impulsive decision to go looking for a stranger in the snowstorm. Was it a mistake? Of course it wasn't, as Mr. Richards was now snoring fitfully. All through the interminable night Larry and I were crammed together in that bag. It was the first time I'd had a powerful marine holding me in his arms. Thankfully, it would also be the last.

The snow did stop and the sun did come out. What had been our nightmare the night before was now beautiful: a new day. No wind, no cold. Even my toe was slightly better. In the light, we could see where we had strayed. We were only ten feet from the trail.

Bobby Richards woke up in a blur, bewildered. Who were we? What had happened? Where was he? He didn't remember a thing. We packed everything up and hiked out. At Whitney Portal, a ranger and his pack animal were waiting for us, along with Bobby Richard's wife and his stepson. He'd never signed up for the climb, but we had, so when we didn't make it down the previous night they began assembling a search team. For us, not him.

The ranger thanked us for saving the elderly man's life. So did Bobby Richard's wife and his stepson. He would have died on the mountain, surely, if we hadn't rescued him. He lost his old Speed Graphic but kept his life.

My good friend Bobby Richards never said a thing. He just disappeared with his family, never volunteering a thank-you. He never sent a note. I was angry at first. Larry and I had risked our own lives to save this thankless man. But in time, I thought better. I had gone up Mount Whitney to challenge myself physically. Instead, I'd faced a challenge of far greater consequence, one that had little to do with reaching the summit and everything to do with what was a really important tome.

My father would have done the same thing. Instead of looking after ourselves, we risked life and limb to help a stranger. I knew how proud it would make him feel, and I couldn't wait to get to a phone and tell him the story. He would no doubt curse the foolish hiker, who, like so many who trek into nature unprepared, not only put himself at risk but also jeopardized the lives of those who attempted to save them.

On the drive back to LA, I remembered those days my father and I spent on my weekend visits in his apartment, wrestling on the floor of his living room. He'd tackle me and tickle me and pin me down, forcing me to maneuver my way out of his grip. "A Goldsmith never gives up," he'd say, and he was right: no matter how strong he was, I managed to get out from his clutches. When I was pinned, he pressured me to figure my way out. It was all a lesson about perseverance. It was a lesson I utilized on Whitney. I was a Goldsmith. And I didn't give up.

If You Can't Move On,
at Least You Can Move

After returning from the mountain, I was determined to get my own place. Living on my friend Koenig's couch for the past month had become a health hazard that rivaled Whitney. I needed my own space, one I didn't share with a roommate or bedbugs. But with slim job prospects, I couldn't afford much. I couldn't even afford to repair my own car.

"Jono, I may have something of interest to you."

Evelyn Amie wasn't a booking agent. She was a friend of my stepfather's (with whom I had come to terms) who had lived in Los Angeles and owned some rental properties throughout the city and the Valley. She knew I didn't have a place to live, was short on cash, and was overstaying my welcome over at Chez Koenig. Evelyn also had a problem with a renter. I seemed like the solution. Win-win.

"I have to evict a tenant from this house I have in the Valley," she said. "Would you like to live there and just look after the property?"

"How much?"

"Free."

"What's the catch?"

"He's threatened to come back and burn the house down," she said. "I don't think it's anything I really have to worry about, but still . . ."

Well, no. It wasn't something that Evelyn had to worry about. It was something that I would have to worry about. Still, it was an incredible deal, in theory. My own pad! No rent! Small fire hazard.

"Absolutely," I told her, accepting the offer without even seeing the place. "I always loved the country."

Then I went to check out the place. The property was on Valleyheart Drive, in North Hollywood, out near Coldwater Canyon. Up the path, I noticed a barn in the back with stalls— for horses, no doubt. The home itself was small, a caretaker's house. The place must have been a farm, I thought. I circled around the back. And that's where I found them.

Five cement troughs. Pools, really. Like pools on a fish farm, but not for fish. For frogs, I learned. I'd been given the keys to an abandoned frog farm. I opened the front door of what years ago must have been the caretaker's house, walked into the living room, and got a sense of Evelyn's pyromaniac tenant's design style. The walls of the home had been plastered with cutouts from *Black Silk Stockings*, a nudie magazine. Everywhere I looked, a collage of scraps adhered to the wall: a flash of breast, skin, teased hair, plastic high heels, cleavage.

Okay. Who was this guy? How hostile was he? What had he been doing here? The scatterings of flesh from the magazine pages hung on the walls were reminiscent of keepsakes of sociopathic characters in horror films, serial killers, true sadists. How serious was he? What was he after? Would he really come back?

The country didn't look so good anymore. I searched the caretaker's house for weapons, for booby traps, any signs of madness. I inspected the closets, the cabinets, expecting to find a prisoner here on the frog farm, perhaps with handcuffs or hog ties or other instruments of depravity. I'd stepped into the former den, surely, of a mad and dangerous man. Then I noticed the window. From the outside of the home, I had seen a window on the second floor. It was small, with wooden panes. On the inside, the window did not exist. On the wall, there was nothing but cold stucco. A fake window?

On second thought, living on my own was great, but it was time to get a roommate.

I called Nick Colasanto, another actor friend, who would later go on to play Coach on the show *Cheers*. At the time, Colasanto had been complaining about how broke he was, just like the rest of us. He was always behind on his rent.

"Nick, I found a place in the country for us to live," I said.

"What's it like, kid?"

"Oh, it's beautiful. It's an old frog farm. You'll love it."

"An old frog farm? What the fuck does that mean?"

"I don't know. There are little cement ponds, but they're empty. We can't swim in them, but come summer, we can wade around. And it's got two bedrooms."

"What's the rent?"

"There is no rent."

"I'll be right over with my stuff," he said, and half an hour later I watched Colasanto's Buick Century pull up, plowing through the weeds that I was pretty sure covered what was once the driveway.

"Lovely," he said, getting out of the car and taking a long, sweeping look around. Together, we loaded all his worldly possessions—two whole boxes' worth—into the caretaker's house. It was late in the day and soon the late afternoon sky had faded. The sun dropped over the Pacific, the chill and darkness of night cooled the Valley, and the stucco caretaker's house was now ice-cold. Where was the heater? We looked for a fireplace, but the rooms were all bare. We looked for a furnace. There was none. The frog farm was no more insulated than the broken-down shed I had built for Rita.

I guess that's the cost of free.

Without chairs, a couch, a source of heat, a television, a radio, or any source of entertainment, Nick and I had nothing to do and no way to keep warm. We stripped the old blinds from the windows and wrapped the ratty drapes around ourselves. The living room was freezing. We could see each other's breath in front of us as if we were smoking cigars. There was only one chair, which we took turns using. Outside, we heard the howl of coyotes, shrieking and cackling like small children. They sounded like they had us surrounded.

Colasanto started muttering about a host of Italian superstitions. He introduced strange words like *fatuta,* a spell, or the *malocchio,* the Italian evil eye, and the various remedies to protect himself from bad omens, like keeping hats off of beds to prevent imminent death. When a coyote bayed at particularly close range, Colasanto sat up and made an announcement.

"We need a fucking watchdog."

The next day, we went to the pound looking for the largest and most imposing dog they had. We took home a Weimaraner and named him Hey Boy, after Richard Boone's Chinese aide on *Have Gun—Will Travel*. He was big. He was imposing. And he was afraid of his own shadow. He was no help, but he was sweet and as in need of a home as we were.

Huddled in the thin, ratty window dressings, I felt like a failure. My career had regressed from promising actor to garbage truck driver. I was broke, hungry as always, and now cold and at risk of being incinerated in my sleep. But misery loves company, and Nick and I were in the same boat. I knew he was a wonderful guy, and I am thankful that some years later, when he got his break on *Cheers*, the American public got to know what a wonderful guy he was too.

He was famous for his pasta. At least that's what he told me. I don't know why. It was okay. But the work provided its warmth, so at least I could leave the curtains behind. I was his sous chef, slicing garlic, peeling tomatoes. As he boiled the water, we'd reminisce about our latest disaster. Since we couldn't get any acting gigs, we posed as house painters during the day. We had no technique whatsoever. Everything ran or curdled. We lost every job we ever had, usually by noon. Obviously, we had no references.

We'd take his car, a wagon that would usually overheat by the time we reached the top of Mulholland Drive, the unofficial dividing line between Hollywood and the Valley. We stashed jugs of water in the sagebrush to feed the radiator. More than once, we coasted down Laurel Canyon into Hollywood with steam spewing from under the hood.

I was the gopher, running to give supplies to the clueless lead painter.

"Nick, you don't know what you're doing," I implored him as he mixed enamel and acrylic together. "You can't do that."

"Keep your voice down," he'd whisper. "They don't know."

After a while, he'd step back dramatically and look upon his work as though it were an artistic masterpiece. The clients never seemed to understand his vision, to put it mildly.

"You don't recognize talent!" Nick would shout. Like the rest of our lives: another failed audition.

"C'mon, kid, let's get out of here," he'd say to me. "They obviously don't recognize genius when they see it."

By the time we were making our nightly pasta, we couldn't stop laughing, imagining the paint still dripping, turning someone's bushes blue.

We thought that frog farm was haunted. Sometimes, I heard strange voices in the night. Had the tenant finally come back to start the fire and burn the whole thing down? Then I'd be not only a failure but a dead failure. But as I'd pad through the creaking house, I'd realize it was Nick mumbling to himself.

"Those people just don't know how to treat artists," he'd mutter, and I'd laugh. Maybe the pasta wasn't so bad after all. In those moments, we were all right.

Nick liked the ladies as much as I did. One day, I came home to find Nick sitting on our only chair. In the front yard. In his boxer shorts. He was trying to get a suntan for a big date he had lined up for that night. He was agitated.

"You got any dough?" he asked.

I saved all my change in a coffee can. I counted it out and was glad to offer my buddy everything I had: twelve bucks. It was certainly enough for him to arm himself with his secret weapon: a bottle of Christian Brothers Brandy.

"Tell me about her, Nicky!"

His excitement was palpable and it was rubbing off on me. It had been a little while for Nicky and I was happy for him.

"Well, she's no kid, maybe midforties. But she's a knockout. She's married, but her husband's out of town on a big case, like, a murder case or something."

A case? Wait a second . . .

"Jesus, Nicky! A cop? Are you sure about this?"

"Of course I'm sure. I'm not passing up an opportunity like this. What do you think, I'm nuts?"

I was starting to.

"Nicky," I said slowly and emphatically. "Cops. Carry. Guns."

"Leave me alone," he said, waving me away and getting back to his rays. "He's in Ohio on a case."

He shaved, drenched himself in some fine Italian aftershave, and was off, arriving at his lady lover's with flowers and Christian Brothers Brandy in hand. All was going well, except for her fox terrier. It was barking, nipping, driving them crazy, and spoiling the mood.

"Honey," said Nicky, "I can't perform like this."

She put the terrier in the bathroom, where Nick's clothes were neatly hung. They danced, feeling no pain. Nicky was in ecstasy. She pulled out a mat from the closet and laid it on the floor, saying she didn't want to denigrate her husband by using the bed. That's very admirable, Nicky thought.

And then Nicky noticed something: She double-locked the front door.

"What's up?" he asked suspiciously.

"You never know, Nicky."

"Never know what? You said your husband was in Cleveland."

"Well, he is. But he's a very suspicious guy. Sometimes he sends his friends to drop by and check on me. Oh, he's a nasty, jealous man, Nicky."

Suddenly, there was a mechanical clicking sound.

"Oh my God, Nick. That's him. He's the only one who can open the garage door. He'll kill us both. Climb out the window. Now."

"Get my clothes," whispered Nicky.

She ran to the bathroom and threw open the door. The dog had shredded his clothes to nothing. She threw the scraps at him and implored him to jump out the window, promising it was a garden apartment, only one floor up. The husband was nearing the stairs. She threw a pair of leotards at Nicky and he grabbed his white bucks with the lifts.

"Jump, Nicky."

"I'll fucking die."

"You will if you don't jump!"

He leapt and landed in the bushes, leotards and bucks in hand, as the husband entered the kitchen. Nicky squeezed into the leotards and white bucks with the lifts. He must have looked like one of the frogs from the farm, with his legs thinned by the tights and his belly hanging over the waistband. He had no shirt, just his shiny Italian medallions dangling around his neck.

He started inching his way through the foliage and down the hedgerows, trying to stay out of sight, when a cop car shined a light on him.

"Over here, honey," they called over the bullhorn. Nick was taken to the Hollywood police station, and if it wasn't for a good friend bailing him out, they would have taken my roommate to the funny farm for a twenty-four-hour psychiatric evaluation.

The Only Way to Get Experience Is to Have Experiences

Do you know where the audition is for *Gunsmoke?*" I asked, peering into an empty room at CBS Studio City. I'd been called in for a role, though didn't know which. I was wearing my blue suit and black Oxford shoes again, looking like an insurance adjuster, while others were wearing Hawaiian shirts and flip-flops.

"This is it," the secretary said.

"What are my sides?" I asked, looking around for the scripts. The audition rooms I'd been in were routinely cattle calls filled with actors.

"There are no sides," she said. "The role of Kyle, the lead, is yours."

I tried to conceal the jubilation building inside me. A starring role, and the first of 350 to follow.

"Mr. Daniels would like to see you," the lady said.

Marc Daniels was a famous television director, and the force behind shows including *I Love Lucy*, *Where's Raymond?*, and, later, *The Golden Girls*. A few days earlier, I had been reading for a part on *Ben Casey*, another show, and he'd been sitting on a bench in the room, working on a script. He must have heard me and cast me without an audition.

"Are you at liberty, son?" he said, asking if my schedule was free enough to take the role.

"Yes, sir," I said, leaving out the only other job I had, which was driving the garbage truck I had parked outside the studio. I used it to get myself to auditions.

"Great, glad to have you on board," he said, grabbing my hand and shaking it. I was ecstatic. As always, I wanted to race to the closest pay phone to call my father.

"Oh, one more thing," Daniels said as I was heading hurriedly toward the door. "You know how to ride a horse, son?"

"Like the wind, sir," I said without breaking stride, anxious to get out of there before someone changed their mind.

I didn't know how to ride a horse. I'd never ridden one. I sat on a pony at the zoo when I was a small child. But after struggling for so long, I couldn't let a horse get in the way of my first real role. Besides, how hard would it be to ride a horse? I was going to find out.

I tried to learn. I called around to the riding stables in Los Angeles, desperate to take a few lessons, but the monsoons had arrived. With all the rain, there was so much mud that nobody would rent out a horse. Still, how hard could it be? I arrived on set one bright morning at the Columbia Ranch without an hour of riding time logged and heard loud, menacing rumblings from inside a semitrailer. It rocked from side to side.

"What's the ruckus?" I said to a grip, trying to feign some cowboy vernacular.

"Nothing, kid. The horses just want to run," he said. The words of the script flashed in my mind: "Kyle vaults on horse and rides through the night." I was Kyle.

Suddenly, it was time for my scene. I was nervous. Okay, I was so shaky the grips had to help me. They boosted me up into the saddle.

"Where'd they get this lox?" I heard someone snicker. I was then given the reins and left to make good on my assurance that I knew how to ride. However, this horse clearly hadn't reviewed the script. And those bastards know when you're afraid. And off he went.

"Pull him around!" Daniels called, prompting two cowboys to chase after the horse and rider.

The crew was cracking up, laughing at me. I had to control this fucking horse. And I couldn't. "Turn him around," everyone yelled. I pulled so damn hard I thought I would break his neck, but he did run in a circle. Right around the director and his camera. Each time I circled out of control, Daniels would follow me with his narrowing eyes.

"Like the wind, eh?" he muttered. I will never forget the look on his face.

Okay, I couldn't ride a mule. But I'd gotten the part. All told, I appeared in sixteen episodes of *Gunsmoke,* and then most of the other popular Westerns of the day: *Bonanza, The High Chaparral,* and *The Virginian,* as well as *Hang 'Em High* with Clint Eastwood. I may hold the record for falling off more horses than anyone else in Hollywood. And once you can stay on, there're saddle sores. They are a very real thing. On *The High Chaparral,* I went to work with Kotex pads on my ass. I still left blood in the saddle.

Eventually, I did learn to ride. A wonderful old cowboy named Don House, who was Gary Cooper's double, took pity on me. We became good friends and I spent many days on his ranch getting far more comfortable in the saddle than I was on my *Gunsmoke* debut. But that day on *Gunsmoke* . . .

"*Cut!*" yelled the director.

Allow Yourself a
Very Wide Margin of Error

My speaking-role debut was less than auspicious as well. I was an extra on *The Doctors*, one of the longest-running shows on television. I received some fan mail; they decided they had a rising star on their hands. They gave me one line.

"Doctor, she has a contusion on her ankle."

I practiced. I had forty different dramatic renditions. After all, I had been to the most prestigious acting school in the East. I alerted friends and family from coast to coast: I would be heard for the first time, live, NBC, Friday at two thirty. I was so ready.

My moment came, and I stepped up to the star of the show. And went completely blank. I was like a deer in the headlights, frozen. It felt like days. But then I said it. My first line ever:

"Doctor, her left ankle is corroded."

Live television. No second takes. I didn't wait to get fired. I just walked out.

*C*ut!"

There it was again. Fred De Cordova, the director of *My Three Sons,* shouted it after I flubbed my lines. I had been cast as a paparazzo and couldn't get the sequencing down. The star of the show was Fred MacMurray, playing a widower, and our episode featured Dana Wynter in a guest appearance. In the script, MacMurray's character was having an illicit lunch with Wynter, who played an heiress. My job was to sneak up on them, snap a few pictures, give my lines, and disappear.

The set had been converted into an elegant restaurant, and the table had been wrapped in fine white linen and set with freshly cut flowers and sparkling crystal wineglasses. Along with the shine of the crystal, I could see the rich patina of MacMurray's hair and the exquisite beauty of Wynter, looking radiant in her elegant beige dress. I had the photo man's attire and props: a vest for lenses and batteries and film and flashbulbs and who knows what else.

I wanted to get familiar with the props before shooting. After all, I was a method actor.

"It's nothing really, just an old Speed Graphic," the prop man told me, handing me the camera. "Nothing to it."

"Um, okay . . . ," I said.

"Here, look," he said impatiently. "This is simple. All you have to do is switch the plate, deliver the line, put the plate back in, take the picture, deliver your second line, expel the flashbulb, and then leave."

It was a dizzying amount of information to absorb, and even more so when I was as nervous as I was. He tried to explain further, but the sound of the director's bullhorn broke his concentration.

"All right, let's take this . . ."

The prop man placed a camera bag on my shoulder.

"Your bulbs and plates are in the bag," he said, ushering me to the stage.

I was confused. Nervous again. Do what with the plate? Then deliver the lines? What, what, what were the lines?

The first take was a dud. I couldn't remember the damn first line. Sitting at the table, Fred MacMurray, the Hollywood star, waited patiently across from the vixen Wynter.

"Let's take it again," the director said.

I got back into position, adjusting the camera bag on my shoulder and feeling the familiar nervous sweat coating my body.

"Action!"

Wait, what were the fucking lines again? Did I press the plate first?

"Cut!"

Over at the table, I noticed Wynter looking over my way, sympathetic, like I was a helpless child. She must have had children of her own, I thought. I was humiliated. My body was drenched.

"Mop him down," the director called, and soon the makeup lady appeared, blotting the sweat from my forehead. This measure, however, wasn't enough.

"Can you get him changed and put some shields in his shirt, for Christ's sake?"

Shields?

The wardrobe lady returned.

"Hopefully, this will help you," she said, lifting my arms to place the pads under my armpits to keep rivulets from dripping down my shirt.

"Can we please get this before lunch?" the director called. "Action!"

I walked out and crushed the line, delivering it perfectly. Now it was time to take the picture. I walked over to the table, mastering the sequence. Just when I got in range, I put the camera to my face, focused the lens just so, put my finger on the camera, and pressed the button.

The wrong fucking button.

The blast of the flashbulb sounded like a mortar round had exploded. Instead of pushing the button to take the picture, I had pushed the button to expel the goddamn flashbulb, and now it was flying. I wanted to jump out into the air and snatch the fucking rocketed bulb, but it was too late—the bulb was high in the air, and my arms were in straitjackets. I could only watch it sail toward the table, over the assembled diners, just missing Fred MacMurray's nose, and landing directly in Dana Wynter's wineglass with a large plop. Of course.

The wine splashed over her beige dress, over the white tablecloth. I had ruined the set.

"*Cut!*"

Once again, I fled. I had a really nice jacket in the dressing room. Instead of going to get it, I just left it there. I got out of the studio. If I couldn't get it right by now, would I ever? I couldn't do this simple thing, and I felt like such a fraud. I wanted to be an actor, and I felt like I couldn't even play a monkey.

ACT II

. . .

In fact, I couldn't play a monkey. I got rejected from playing one of the gorillas in *Planet of the Apes*. I had come to be friends with the director Ted Post after he cast me to play alongside Clint Eastwood in *Hang 'Em High*. Eastwood never talked to me again after the film (a dalliance I had had with his girlfriend in Las Cruces, New Mexico, during filming might have had something to do with it), but I became a lifelong friend of Post's, who thought I'd make a good ape.

"Report in on Monday, three A.M. Makeup and wardrobe," my agent told me. "It's a fairly small part, but you got it, and it runs through the picture."

I was thrilled. Playing a minor ape didn't necessarily forge a clear path to major roles in films, but it was finally a steady income. The film was a long contract, spanning several months, and the best part was the overtime coming my way. Those ape costumes took hours to create in makeup and wardrobe, and, along with special effects, it guaranteed a very good year. Again, I called my father.

"Poppa, I'm going to be a star," I gushed. "I'm playing a monkey in *Planet of the Apes*."

He was so thrilled. How supportive.

"Great, kid. I always knew you had it."

I had hardly hung up the phone when it rang again. It was my agent.

"J-J-J-Jono? What . . . color are your . . . eyes?" he stammered.

"B-B-B-Blue?" I stammered back.

"Sh-sh-shit. All the apes have b-b-brown eyes," he said. "No time to get lenses."

Jesus, I thought. Thirty years old and I couldn't even play a fucking monkey! A tough break, for sure, but a punishment I had become heartbreakingly familiar with. Like the time I was cast to play alongside Danny DeVito but was too tall. Or the time I wasn't tall enough, and my agent stuffed the soles of my shoes with gobs of wet toilet paper in the studio's bathroom. I could hardly walk. My calves were spasming. I made it to the reading hobbling. After the audition the director said, "He's great, just put him in lifts."

One time, after the umpteenth rejection, flub, or failure, I found myself lost on Wilshire Boulevard. As I walked, I passed a cemetery, small and odd-looking. I found an entrance on Glendon Avenue and walked in, shuffling aimlessly among the tombstones. Then I stumbled on a familiar name. Norma Jeane Mortenson, whom we knew as Marilyn Monroe. She'd become so famous, so lusted after, and yet she'd committed suicide, unable to cope with her own pain. Just like Inge, she'd surrendered to her own dark thoughts. And I felt like such a worthless, inadequate failure. Perhaps this was the way to make the pain of rejection disappear. Maybe dying would be my lot in life.

For a while, it kind of was. But fortunately, I didn't need to kill myself. In fact, I learned I could make a decent career having others do it for me.

It's Better to Die Onstage
Than to Not Get Onstage at All

I may well have been killed more than anyone else during my time in Hollywood. I was pushed off a roof as a drug dealer in *T. J. Hooker*. I was thrown off a roof as a drug addict in *Dallas* and was tossed off another roof or two in *The Streets of San Francisco* (and also, in a later episode, drowned in a bathtub by a gang dressed up as nuns). I was mowed down by a machine gun, and once I was electrocuted. I was blown up by dynamite and run over by a car. Several times. I was killed so many times that Leonard Katzman, a close friend and director, refused to use me anymore.

"I can't do it, Jono," Katzman said. "Maybe if you come back as a blond or something?"

He was joking. But I wasn't. That afternoon, I went out and had my hair dyed blond. I came back the next day, got the part, and got whacked again. I don't know what it was about me. I guess people just liked seeing me die.

"It doesn't hurt, does it?" director Don Siegel said, after I got shot in the head by John Wayne for the seventh time in just a few hours. Don Siegel had become famous directing a cult picture called *Invasion of the Body Snatchers*. I was on the set of *The Shootist,* the last film Wayne ever made. I had just crashed through a glass window to shoot the Duke. Of course, I missed. He didn't. I was rolling around on the ground in pain, where Mr. Wayne was to give me the coup de grâce.

Wayne was huge, towering over me, firing a prop pistol from six feet away. The gun had blanks, but out of camera view, there was a prop man with an air gun who fired pellets filled with fake blood. So, every time Wayne shot me, the prop man fired a blood pellet at my head, which stung and left a nasty welt. Now, after seven times, they were wondering if it hurt.

"Just a little, Mr. Siegel," I said, seeing double. I was about to pass out.

"That's great! Okay, everybody, let's take it again," Siegel called, and Wayne shot me for the eighth time. My head was throbbing and I could hardly see, my head riddled with blood pellets.

Siegel got out of his chair to inspect the set. He looked down at the welts on my head.

"How much they paying you for this, kid?" he asked.

"Seven hundred." I winced.

"Well, if it makes you feel any better, most of the people the Duke shoots turn out to be stars."

How nice, I thought.

"All right," Siegel yelled. "One more time! For safety!"

The Duke did shoot me. And I did become a star. But I'd have to wait thirty-five years. In the meantime, my death run continued. I was pushed off a boat in some mucky swamp, shot too many times to count, strapped to the electric chair, and hanged from the gallows in *Cutter's Trail* by Joseph Cotten, who, incidentally, had just had false front teeth fitted. As a result, he had quite a bit of trouble with my character's name and his line.

"Any lastht requesthtsth, Jesstheee Bowen?" he asked, again and again, tears rolling down his cheeks. We had to keep taking it and taking it because, frankly, an outlaw with a noose around his neck shouldn't be laughing so hard.

Then I was buried alive.

I'd been cast in *The Law & Harry McGraw,* a television show, in a leading role. I played Flash, a Broadway star and bon vivant known to cavort with numerous showgirls. I don't remember how I was killed, but what's the difference? Dead is dead, so we had to do a funeral scene. Instead of shooting the funeral on set, the production had rented out a decrepit funeral parlor in Pasadena.

Inside, the place was musty, with dark gray drapes and caskets all over the place. I was dressed in a snappy suit, of course, with a flower in my lapel and a pocket square—Flash was a flashy guy. We were late shooting and about to head into overtime, so the grips had to find a coffin quickly. I had to jump in.

"Open up that one," the assistant director said.

The grip lifted the top of the coffin and shrieked. Inside was a woman, elderly, small, and quite dead. She was wearing a gray dress.

"Sir," I mumbled respectfully, "can we please get another coffin?"

I looked questioningly at the assistant director, whom I didn't especially like anyway.

"Just get in the fucking coffin."

The grips reached in and yanked the woman out, and in I went. I could smell the toxic traces and stench of death, the formaldehyde, old and stale. With the cover closed, I couldn't help but imagine my own death. I could hear the actresses talking about my character through the coffin's lid, the showgirls approaching one by one, speaking in nasal voices, as if they'd all been cast in a Long Island nail salon.

"Oh, Flash, you were the best."

"We're never going to forget you, Flash."

I stared up at the lid of the coffin, so dark and confining. Would it be like this? I wondered, letting my mind race while hyperventilating slightly. Who would show up at my funeral? What would they say?

I'd killed myself onscreen a few times, but my most emotional death happened in *Go Tell the Spartans*, still considered a cult picture. I starred opposite Burt Lancaster. The challenge was the sound. The location was next to Magic Mountain amusement park, and every time the director called action, along came the roller coaster and the shrieks of the tourists. The soundtracks were all messed up. I ended up dubbing the most dramatic scene of my life, my suicide scene, in an empty studio. No actors, no props. Just an empty studio. It came out all right. The New York *Daily News* said it was an Academy Award–worthy performance.

I had mastered the art of dying. The trick was to take the last image I saw and hold on to that scene in my mind, watching it dim, trying to get it back, savoring the last vision of life. A twitch of the leg or mouth never hurt either. I mastered the eye flutter and gasping too. But dying all those times really affected me. These scenes didn't help my melancholia either. It was hard not to think about the fragility of existence and transience of life when you were the one it was constantly being taken away from.

If You Want Something Done Right, Do It Yourself

Mr. Lancaster, can I have your autograph?" the boy said. He had a butch haircut and a skinny frame. He'd sidled up to the booth in the Ranch House restaurant, a diner in Valencia where Burt Lancaster and I had been meeting regularly for breakfast. I had been in awe of Lancaster since I saw him in *The Crimson Pirate* when I was a kid. And then there I was, actually costarring with one of my idols. In *Go Tell the Spartans,* he played Major Barker and I played Sergeant Oleonowski.

Burt had an active and eclectic mind. He was an opera devotee as well as a boxing fan—he was a physical specimen himself. Like many stars I had met, he was tired of the ongoing assault of fans. As we sat having breakfast at the diner, he looked down at this grinning young boy asking for an autograph.

"No," he said gruffly.

I couldn't believe it. The kid must have been seven, eight years old. How do you turn down a child?

The boy frowned with sadness, looking confused.

"Tell your mother to leave you alone," Burt said. "Just go and be a little boy."

The child turned away, upset, and scurried away from the table.

"What was that all about?" I asked.

"This kid was born five years ago," Burt said. "He has no idea who Burt Lancaster is. His mother put him up to it."

Stars do get tired of a demanding public. There's a famous story about Paul Newman, who seldom gave autographs. Once, a woman bugged him to show her his baby blues. Exasperated, he said, "Sure, show me your tits and I'll show you my eyes."

I looked over. In a booth in the back of the diner, I saw the young boy and his mother. Sure enough, she seemed more disappointed than him.

I remember a game Lancaster and I once invented. We were on set, waiting around for our scene, desperate to kill time. We decided to see how many names for "vagina" we could come up with. In total, we spent at least half an hour going back and forth, soon hitting five, ten, and more. We stopped at thirty-seven. The most unusual was "quatiffi." That was Burt's offering, which impressed me, though I have no idea where it came from.

Your Greatest Teacher
Won't Be Found in School

I am looking for a crazy motherfucker, and I think you are perfect," Fernando Lamas told me. He was directing an episode of *The Rookies* and called me in to meet with him at 20th Century Fox. We were up in the anonymous office used by visiting directors, with the typical posters on the walls and head shots lying on the desk. Fernando, though, was impeccable, wearing a jacket with an elegant monogrammed silk shirt and loafers. He had a deep tan and luxurious, shining hair. He was the epitome of a movie star. Lamas was a product of invention, and the inventor was him. He wasn't the most well-known Hollywood star in life, but after his death, when the comedian Billy Crystal started to imitate him with his hilarious skit "Fernando's Hideaway" and the whole "You look marvelous" thing, he became renowned to all.

Fern, as I came to know him, had an intense energy and an extremely interesting background. He'd come to Hollywood from Argentina, and as far as I could tell he came from modest means. His real name sounded a lot like royalty to me—Fernando Álvaro Lamas y de Santos. And yet, there was another side to him—a tough, raw side. He could be crude and fearless. He was a middleweight boxing champion in Argentina, a country famous for its machismo and its fabulous pugilists, including Luis Firpo, the heavyweight and so-called Wild Bull of the Pampas, whose fights I would follow on the radio, and the middleweight legend Carlos Monzón, whom my father and I would watch brawling on television.

Looking back on Fernando now, I wonder how we developed such a lasting friendship and how he came to have the incredible influence he would have on my career. I think it was Fern's overt machismo I admired so much—perhaps because underneath the layers of my own self, that was something I didn't have. At least not yet.

I remember him telling me about being on the set of *100 Rifles*, the 1969 picture directed by Tom Gries starring Burt Reynolds and Raquel Welch. During the filming, one of the crew members was getting pushy with Raquel Welch. Fernando noticed her discomfort and did what all guys would like to think they would do but don't always have the courage to do. He didn't care about getting fired. He didn't give it a second thought. On horseback, he charged to the top of the hill and challenged the first assistant to combat.

"Don't you ever behave like that to a lady," he admonished. "She's my friend and you're nothing but a fucking coward."

Then he reared his horse dramatically and galloped off. Fern was really like that. Honor and chivalry were important to him, perhaps more so than anything else. I remember one argument we had, about something so minor I don't remember what it was. But instead of arguing the point with me, whatever it was, or raising his voice to scream like so many of us do, he put his hands up and got into a boxer's crouch.

"You want to hit me?" he said, pawing a lead left in the air. "Do you think you can do it? You want to fight with Fernando? I was in the fucking ring. I was a boxer, you know. You got the guts?"

Not surprisingly, Fern and I became fast friends. We even formed a production company together, calling it Bravura Productions, jumping immediately into a fun, endless cycle of talking projects, development, casting, all aspects of production, whom we would use as crew, and, most important, our choices for leading ladies. I would star; Fernando would direct. We spent hours designing and redesigning our film logo and even secured two hundred thousand dollars in seed money. But mostly, it was just one laugh-filled lunch after another.

He was Latino, and the most important part of the day for him was lunch. He insisted I join him and Esther Williams, his wife, to eat with them at their home every day. If I missed a day, he'd get upset and call me.

"Something wrong?" he'd say, hurt. "We were counting on you coming for lunch today."

"Well, Fern, I had things to do," I'd say.

"Oh, are we no longer friends?"

He was a demanding friend and a master of passive aggression, so I usually made it for lunch. I'd find my way to their home near the Beverly Hills Hotel, and in the driveway there would be Fern's Rolls-Royce, which he never drove, always insisting Esther drive him around. The house itself was a mansion in miniature, with brick and stone in the old Hollywood style. Inside, the place was elegant enough—piss elegant, I'd say—for Fern could be a cheap bastard, and the sofas and tables and chairs had that dated and dusty look, probably taken from struck sets. He'd been acting in Hollywood since the forties, and every once in a while these old-time legends—Rock Hudson, James Doolittle, Barbara Rush—would stop by and join us, as would Dane Clark, one of my heroes, and Anthony Newley. And, of course, numerous other movers and shakers.

Esther loved to cook. She had a heartfelt midwestern way about her, and despite her roles in film (she was once the highest-paid female actress in the world), she was really known throughout the nation as a swimmer. As a teenager, she'd set numerous swimming records and won the national championship for the one-hundred-meter freestyle in 1939, as well as contributing to several relay team wins. She was a shoo-in for the Olympics in 1940, but the games were abruptly canceled with the war in Europe raging, and instead of becoming a star athlete, she became an entertainer in water shows. She helped put synchronized swimming on the map.

As a younger man, I remember watching the choreographed swimming scenes in films like *Neptune's Daughter*. Before Esther's movie run, she costarred with Johnny Weissmuller in Billy Rose's Aquacade during the New York World's Fair from 1939 to 1940. Weissmuller, another great swimmer, went on to play Tarzan. They swam in perfect harmony.

Once, Ricardo Montalbán starred opposite her as a great swimmer. One small problem: He couldn't swim. So they built an underwater ramp, and all through the film, while he was swimming, he was actually walking. Fernando called him "the sinker of *Fantasy Island.*"

It was wild to me that Esther and Fernando had such a tiny swimming pool, probably the smallest in Beverly Hills. The pool was so small it was impossible to swim a lap of more than two or three strokes. I never asked her about the pool, just relished her sweet nature and the delicious handmade empanadas she baked for Fern, the fresh soups and endless courses that would come out of her kitchen every day for those elaborate lunches. Fern insisted on eating like royalty, and lunch was a formal affair: starched tablecloth, polished silver, crystal glasses and goblets for the wine. The purpose of these lunches was to talk business, to develop our shows and films, but we rarely got that far, passing the bottles of Malbec from Argentina, telling stories, and howling with laughter.

Fern liked the sun, liked to feel the warmth covering his face, and he'd retreat to the backyard after the meal and sit in his chaise longue to absorb the rays. Before joining him one day, I helped Esther with the dishes. I was becoming like an adopted son to them.

"Esther, why does he like me so much?" I asked.

"Because you make him laugh," she said.

Fern made me laugh too. After lunch, I'd pull up a chair and sit next to him on the lawn. We spoke about everything, but I remember hearing about his exploits with women the most. I was in awe of this man's ability to seduce the world's most beautiful women. Like many stars, he was a perennial at the Beverly Hills Hotel. Once, after a few guests complained about the loud shrieking sounds coming from his room, the house detective knocked on the door.

"Mr. Lamas, are you all right?" he asked.

"Yes, Butch," he said. "It's nothing. I've got Lana in here."

"Okay, Mr. Lamas. Just checking."

He was with Lana Turner, a goddess to be sure, the star of *Peyton Place* and *The Bad and the Beautiful,* among so many other films.

"'Johnny,' she would yell like a banshee, and when she was climaxing, her feet would flap like a bird," he told me.

Then he'd mention his love affair with Anita Ekberg, the star of Federico Fellini's *La Dolce Vita.* The list was endless. I was spellbound.

"Fernando, how many people in Hollywood did you fuck?" I once asked.

After a moment of careful consideration, he stated, matter-of-factly, "I think I got most of them."

He never cheated on Esther, though, and I wondered in part if it was because of the way she treated him. She catered to him like he was a baronial prince, and he loved her almost as much as he loved himself. He could not be bothered or placed in discomfort for even an instant. Once, I remember Esther wanted to leave the city and go camping in the High Sierra.

"I'm not going up there with the fucking bugs," he announced.

"Come on, Fern. I'll pack your favorite champagne and pâté."

"If you insist. But I will do nothing. You've got to do everything."

"Don't I always?"

It was true. She packed up the Rolls-Royce. She packed the picnic basket, stuffing it with rare viands, caviar, pâté, champagne, and all of his favorite snacks. He reminded her that he would not go without his chaise longue, which she dutifully strapped to the roof of the Rolls. Esther got in the car and started driving, with him bitching in the passenger seat mile after mile like the petulant child he frequently was. Finally, after four hours, they arrived. Fern stood in the middle of the campsite, arms folded, the crest on his jacket gleaming in the Sierra sunset, his embroidered slippers covered with a light layer of dust, much to his chagrin. As usual, he was delivering his orders.

"Esther, set up the tent."

"Yes, Fern."

"Esther, the mosquitoes are bothering me."

"Yes, my darling."

"Esther, I need a fire. I am chilled."

"Okay, darling."

After Esther had lit the fire and hand-fed him his delicacies, the darkness of night had come and they entered the tent, ready for bed. He wouldn't stop moving around inside the tent.

"Esther?"

"Yes, Fern?"

"I can feel every one of these fucking stones," he said, complaining about the ground underneath their quilt.

"Esther, lie still," he said. "Fernando is going to sleep upon you."

And that's what he did. He crawled over and lay on top of his superstar wife, using his beloved as a mattress. I was frequently very uncomfortable with his chauvinism, but it seemed to work for them completely. Everyone who had the privilege of knowing them had stories that were as legendary as Fern and Esther's love for each other.

Fortune Favors the Bold
and the Brash

Fern's playfulness and lack of boundaries were intertwined with his faux nobility. One day, we were on my boat. The other guests around him attended to his every need and hung on his every word as he regaled us with nonstop stories about his early days in Argentina and his hilarious Hollywood escapades. Suddenly, he got quiet. He was staring off at the horizon, looking a bit peaked. He could never appear weak, and he could never be anything but the epitome of class. So, when it was time to be sick, he stood up, approached me, and discreetly inquired, "Which side of your fucking yacht would you like me to use, Johnny?"

I can still see Esther, holding her beloved by his belt and asking him if he wanted an anchovy sandwich. She seemed to enjoy his momentary strife.

"Boy, we could get a lot from the *National Enquirer* for this picture," I said as he hurled for the sixth time. He turned his face to me.

"That is not fucking funny," he said, then angled his head to the side and threw up once again. We all enjoyed his rare moment of vulnerability. We felt a little guilty, but it was hard to contain our laughter.

It was usually Fernando who relished making others squirm. He was a master of manufacturing the awkward moment and using it to disarm and charm all within earshot. One afternoon, we were riding up the elevator in Century City, going to see his lawyer—now mine as well—for our now-struggling Bravura Productions, and we were all jammed in the elevator riding up. He looked like an Italian count, with his ascot and those embroidered slippers.

"Johnny?" he said in a loud voice, turning to me.

The elevator was otherwise quiet, and I cringed at what he would say to embarrass me.

"You know, when I wear these shoes, I always get a blow job," he said.

Good God.

Fernando, please," I begged another time. I had finally been accepted at the very prestigious California Yacht Club. This was years later, after I had started to get a number of steady roles, and I had just been accepted as a member—my first membership to anything other than a gym, so I was on my best behavior in the upper-crust atmosphere. We had driven to the club in the Rolls, with Esther at the wheel like always, and Fern giving the directions.

"Don't embarrass me," I told him in the car.

"I wouldn't do that. Why would I do that, Johnny?" he said, looking aghast and hurt that I would say such a thing.

"Please," I urged, knowing better. "This is important to me, Fernando. It's taken me years to be accepted."

"Okay, Johnny. I will be on my best behavior. I'll be good, Johnny."

It was opening day, and there was a traditional celebration that involved the firing of a cannon. We walked in and saw Commodore Royce, the club president, who came over to greet us. He was wearing white flannels and the obligatory navy blue blazer, the epitome of class and gentility. Just as he stepped within earshot of us, Fern took over, and in his loud, booming voice, as the commodore leaned in to shake our hands and welcome us, he said, "And that, Johnny, is how I fucked a water buffalo right in his ass."

Let It All Hang Out

Fernando left me with so many lessons, particularly the importance of chivalry. He'd invented himself to be a noble, but he was committed to playing the role on and off the screen. Naturally, he'd been married a few times, once to Arlene Dahl (who mothered his son, Lorenzo Lamas), whom he called Paperhead. She was suspicious that he was cheating on her, which of course he was. He told me about a curious incident.

"Johnny, she was having me followed," he said with a mysterious, pointed inflection, pulling his chair closer to mine.

Back then, to get a divorce you had to prove a spouse had committed a foul deed. There were a number of them she could have chosen from. She was suspicious, so Fern was convinced she'd hired a private detective to catch him in flagrante. It was New Year's Eve on the night in question, and the weather had been terrible. A storm front was coming in, and Fern had stayed home for the evening.

"Johnny, I am alone in my mansion, and I, Fernando Lamas, am sitting by the fire naked and drinking a fine Courvoisier," he told me.

Listening to the sounds of the storm, naked in his chair, he heard a noise. It was coming from the tree outside his window.

"I know there is some poor motherfucker outside, and he's up in a tree somewhere," he said. He suspected the man in the branches was the private detective his wife had hired, presumably staking him out with a camera to get evidence of Fern with another woman.

"It's pouring and I feel sorry for this poor bastard," he said. "So I, Fernando Lamas, throw the front door open to the tempest. I say, 'You poor motherfucker, it's New Year's Eve, come down from wherever you are if you're not a coward and have a drink with Fernando.'"

Outside, there was silence. Then came the noise of movement in the branches. He watched the detective climb down carefully from the tree. Moments later, the drenched private eye appeared sheepishly at the front door.

"You want me to take my shoes off, Mr. Lamas?"

"That's perfectly all right, my friend. Come in and join me."

It takes a special kind of guy to sit naked in front of a fire and invite the private detective hired to spy on him in for a drink on New Year's Eve. He was part gentleman and part rascal, though perhaps more of the latter.

I scattered Fernando Lamas's ashes off my boat after he died, accompanied by his family and some friends. He'd been suffering from back pain and thought it was just a nerve or muscle sprain from playing tennis. He refused to see a doctor and insisted on holistic remedies, only to learn when the pain became too much that he had cancer. I can still see it, his embroidered slippers moving gracefully across the teak deck of my boat, him drinking tequila and me listening to tales from his endless library of exploits, a treasure trove that I would mine long after he was gone.

Quality, Not Quantity.
But, Also, Quantity.

Fernando's fearless approach was inspiring to me. I saw how being so blunt could make strangers laugh, and with laughter and directness came a unique, perhaps devilish, way to seduce women. I'm proud of my track record. I'm also not proud of it. I didn't know then about myself what I know now, and here is what I've discovered: The attention, approval, and warmth I always craved from my mother and never received forced me to look for approval in other places—namely, from women. My struggling career was also a part of it. If I couldn't conquer my professional life, I had to conquer something.

I was hungry too. I had a lovely dalliance with Jack Warner's much younger girlfriend, and with one of Groucho Marx's wives. Two congressmen's wives (both Republican), six vegetarians, nine Buddhists, eighteen nurses, sixteen teachers, eleven subs, countless receptionists (even one at an abortion clinic, where I'd come with an aspiring starlet), and one runner-up to Miss Florida, as well as many extras, thirteen players, and one Academy Award winner. I broke Henry Fonda's mistress's bed. Some of the women I pursued were married. Sometimes I'd get lucky and one woman would refer me to another. Many are still friends, even after so many years.

Georgia

She was like a Skidmore girl. She wore penny loafers and a Catholic schoolgirl's pleated skirt. I remember her long legs. She was married to a famous orthopedist to the stars. We ended up in the bathroom of her house, on the floor. Hungry.

Susan

That was the code name I used for her. Susan's real name was Tina Louise. We met at the Actors Studio, a famous acting workshop and the home of method acting. While we were rehearsing for a scene, one thing led to another. She was the most beautiful woman I had ever been with.

She lived off Coldwater Canyon. We always met at her house. She'd leave a message for me—"It's Susan"—and I'd park behind the garage. As I quietly tiptoed through the foliage, the gardeners used to smile at me knowingly. I'd slip into her boudoir through the side door. She'd be waiting naked in the bed. She was beautiful to behold. Simply beautiful.

I really felt rather proud of myself. She was so desired after playing Ginger on *Gilligan's Island*. I would be the envy of all, if they'd known. But it was our wonderful secret. And definitely good medicine for an out-of-work actor. She had such great stamina I was afraid I would have a heart attack by the third or fourth round. I even thought about my obituary. UNKNOWN ACTOR FOUND DEAD AT YOUNG AGE. Surely I'd be mentioned by name this time, though.

"Tina," I'd say, "I'm going to have a heart attack."

She refused to stop. She was a true beauty—tall, elegant, with a cool distance and complete, unfettered surrender.

Afterward, we'd take a shower together. We talked about everything. My wife, her boyfriends, the theater. Sometimes she'd bring me bourbon in bed and allow me to smoke in her boudoir, even though she didn't approve of smoking. One time, when we couldn't go to her house, we found ourselves in the back of my truck, just down the hill from Marlon Brando's house. Tina was a special friend. Those were good times.

Elaine Stritch

She was Ms. Broadway. A huge international star and very flamboyant. She was larger than life, her whiskey voice unforgettable. I remember her walking her dog, staggering through numerous Hollywood dawns before heating leftovers for a champagne-accompanied breakfast in my humble flat. She would wear a pair of high heels, a mink coat, and nothing underneath. She really looked a bit out of place in the semi-slum I lived in, especially in her sunglasses when the sun wasn't completely up. I met her at a party with Gerry O'Loughlin, my dear friend who introduced me to Leo Penn, a prolific television director and Sean's father—which led to a lifetime friendship. He also sponsored me to audition at the Actors Studio. I was just a kid, and I took Elaine back to my apartment. Once, at four in the morning, she made me lamb chops with Roquefort sauce. It was very charming, we laughed often, and we liked each other very much. It was so good, and it was the second time I had it that way. The first time was with Jacqueline.

Jacqueline

She was kept by a famous newsman in a nice apartment around the corner from the Hickory Pit in New York City, a block from the United Nations, where I was living with John Phillip Law, my fellow acting student at the Neighborhood Playhouse. She was petite, elfin, as only a Parisian could be—a gorgeous little thing with a beautiful French accent. I was nineteen. One day, she said, "Would you deliver to my apartment?" I didn't go to school or back to work for two days. She made me lamb chops with Roquefort sauce that, I must admit, will always be better than Elaine Stritch's. She complained about American women and had a charming name for her vagina. She called it her zizi.

Camille

When I was feeling lonely and unfulfilled, I could always go to the studio. Make the rounds, try to make them laugh, and meet up with a couple of the secretaries. At Universal one day, I had a great tryst on the *African Queen,* lying quietly on an empty soundstage, where it had been for years. Monte Davis was a big producer, having worked on many shows, and he was married to a big star. He had a French secretary by the name of Camille, a very classy Parisian woman. We would frequently have lunch at the commissary, which I couldn't have gone to myself. Downstairs, we had a love nest—a tiny room behind the telephone bank where we would get it on. Her murmuring in French and the sound of the studio hubbub just outside of the door was a delightful break in an empty afternoon looking for work.

Three's Company,
a Freeway's a Crowd

Mona and Debbie

And speaking of the French: I came to meet and date a beautiful French model. Actually, she was from the Bronx. I'll call her Mona. She'd strangle me if I told you her name, but here's what I can tell you: She dated the Aga Khan, was a leading model in Paris at six-teen, became a millionaire on her own, and was kept by a cowboy movie star in Hollywood. We had a convenient arrangement. I'd park the garbage truck outside her apartment near the corner of Ol-ive and Fountain, a beautiful Spanish building, and slip up into her apartment. I would take the servants' stairs, as I was fresh off the job and looked it. The apartment had thick old walls. A rough texture. Period furniture. When I came over, she would cook me a steak. We'd watch soap operas and then go at it like rabbits in her bed.

Deborah was Mona's girlfriend. Deborah was married to a well-known director in Florida, and when she came to Los An-geles for a visit, Mona threw a party for her. Mona would throw a party for anyone—any excuse to further her career. I showed up to the party and met Deborah, and we had that magical click. We partied all night, dancing, laughing, feeling no pain. After the guests had left, Debbie and I were deeply in love. Or lust, at the very least. We were all in our underwear dancing around, just floating and high and feeling great for four o'clock on a Monday morning. Soon even my underwear was off. I had always wanted to have a threesome, and, given the circumstances, I thought I had landed the perfect opportunity.

Mona was cleaning up and I followed her into the kitchen.

"Mona," I asked. "Debbie has come over thirty-two hundred miles from Florida to be here, and as a welcome, I would like to borrow the spare room. Would you mind?"

I knew she wouldn't, since Mona always had at least three lovers at all times and never got jealous anyway.

"No, darling, but do me a favor first," she said, scrubbing a few dishes, as the maid had left.

"Happily," I said.

"Take out the garbage."

"*Mais certainement*," I said, grabbing the trash bag and feeling so proud of myself. I had done it! Oh boy! Here I was, dancing around with these two beautiful girls, hugging them both, kissing them and watching them flit about in their underwear. It was the best of beautiful Hollywood. With the garbage bag in my hand, I opened the outside door and headed for the incinerator, so excited for the conquest to come, feeling so complete.

The door shut with an ominous click. Oh fuck. I could feel the cold tiles of the terrazzo floor under my feet, the breeze between my legs. I was stark naked. Turning the handle of Mona's door, I found that I was now locked out.

I knocked on the door.

"Who is it?" Mona said, giggling in her faux French accent.

"Jehovah's Witness," I said. "Let me in!"

I was standing, waiting. I banged. Behind the door, I could hear my lovelies dying with laughter.

I was getting nervous. The sun was coming up. I was seeing this sheet of orange light reflecting in the windows of the sleeping building. Dawn broke, the sun rising over Hollywood and starting to break up the dark, purple clouds. I could hear the sounds of tenants opening windows, walking their dogs, and greeting the new day. Oh Jesus. Under one of the many stucco archways, I saw a dog and a leash, and a pair of guys taking little Fifi for a walk.

I jumped behind a bird of paradise. What was I going to do? Would Mona and Debbie let me back in?

I raced around to the living room window and banged at the glass. I could see them both inside, still in their underwear, holding each other, stoned, howling with laughter, tears running down. Then I heard footsteps and turned.

A neighbor appeared. A man. He was heading to work, just like everyone else.

"Morning," I said, saluting him before I raced out into the street to get to my car. Oh God. Where had I parked? Was it down on Fountain? Or was it on Olive?

Shaking off the hangover, I saw a damp newspaper—the sprinklers had caught us both—grabbed it, and used it as a loincloth to cover my manhood. Then I set out to hunt for my car, hopping from one bird-of-paradise bush to another. The street was becoming busier.

"Good morning," I said to one neighbor with a smile, springing behind the foliage.

"How are you?" I said to another, ducking behind a palm tree. Finally, I spotted my Impala convertible, which I had purchased for three hundred dollars because the roof didn't go up. I was so relieved to see my car, but then it hit me. I had no keys. No wallet, no shoes. I was naked. What was I going to do?

Aha! The hide-a-key! I wondered if it was still there. I was always losing keys, so I stashed a spare under the bumper. I darted out to the car and reached under the rear bumper. Eureka! The key was a bit rusty, but it worked. I retreated to the relative cover of my uncovered convertible Impala.

I turned over the key and headed back to the frog farm, grinning and chuckling to myself. I thought, Oh boy, wait until I get to the gym. Wait until I get into the steam room and tell the guys about Mona and Debbie . . . Even though I had missed my opportunity, I was very proud of myself. I had a great story.

I pulled onto the freeway, the sun now up and the morning commute beginning. I took in the view of Los Angeles, hoping that the other drivers wouldn't look over and take in a view of me, when I heard a startling sound.

Putter.

The car jerked.

Putter, putter.

I looked at my gas gauge. Below empty. Damn it. How long could I last? Two miles? A mile? I eased up on the gas. This was problematic, as I was going uphill. My exit was the next one: Barham Boulevard. If nothing else, I could get out and sprint to a pay phone at my coffee shop and make a desperate call. But whom would I call? And with what money would I make the call? I didn't have a penny, let alone a dime.

Then the car jolted, suffered a final twitch, and croaked in the center lane of US 101, the Hollywood Freeway. Just at the beginning of rush hour in Los Angeles. There I was, stopping traffic in the road-rage capital of the universe, completely naked.

The other cars backed up, horns blared. They inched around me, screaming, giving me the finger. The pileup was instant, enormous. I was sweating. How am I going to get out of here? Ditch the car and run? I could see the headline: UNIDENTIFIED ACTOR [maybe this time I'd get some credit] SPRINTS NAKED DOWN THE 101, ABANDONS CAR, CHASED BY POLICE. But I was immobilized. What could I do?

I turned on the radio—maybe the music would relax me— and that's when I heard the report.

"Massive traffic jam on the 101 and Hollywood Freeway at Highland Avenue," the radio announcer said.

Time seemed to have stood still. Then I heard the sounds. Heavy, swirling, thumping sounds. It was a helicopter, looming above me. Here was our eye in the sky.

On the radio, the traffic man was updating the report by talking to the pilot, who seemed to be having a very good time at my expense.

"I found the problem," he said. "Naked man, middle of the freeway."

I looked up at the helicopter and waved. In the meantime, I was sweating profusely. I wondered how to get out of this trap. Nobody to call. No money. Just imprisoned in my roofless Impala.

Then I heard the sirens. I looked in the rearview. A police car was pulling up beside me on the service road. An old cop with a handlebar mustache made his way to me in the barely cruising traffic, craning his head into the Impala. I smiled back at him, naked as the day I was born, with a ragged, soggy newspaper over my lap.

"Son, have you been drinking?" he asked.

"Yes, Officer, I have been, or I was, but I'm completely sober now. My girlfriend Mona and her friend Debbie, they locked me out of the apartment . . ."

"That's fine. We're going to take you someplace where you can rest, son."

Rest? What does rest mean? A hospital? An insane asylum?

"I-I-I don't need a rest," I told him. "I need a push. I live just over the crest of the hill . . ."

But the cop had heard it all. He turned his head back to the squad car, surrounded by a sea of furious drivers.

"Fred, get the blanket," he hollered to his partner.

The blanket?

In the rearview, I watched the officer walk up to my car, blanket cradled in his arms. I imagined the straitjackets, padlocked doors, white walls. Holy shit!

But wait. This guy . . . this cop . . . he looked . . . familiar.

Oh my God. I knew him! I had just finished playing in a television episode that ended with, what else? My death, this time by electrocution. This dear officer was one of the technical advisers on the show.

"Jono?" he said. And then he started laughing. I smiled sheepishly, still panicking. He told me to put the car in neutral, and he and the other officer got back into their cruiser and pushed me to the exit. I coasted down Barham and found my way to the safety of Floyd Terrace, glad to be home at last.

Every once in a while, I kick myself. Never let a door shut permanently behind you. I could have had that threesome.

There's One Thing
That Never Gets Old . . .

The Psychologist

I saw her in the gym every day. She was a psychologist, and we had a game we would play. At night, I would go over to her place and we'd switch roles. To unwind, Jane would sit in the chair where all her patients usually were, holding a little bell. I would sit across from her in her chair—the doctor's chair. (My mother always wanted me to be a doctor.) Jane would demonstrate the patient's symptoms. She would play the patient and I would play the doctor doing a clinical work-up on her. Every time I made a mistake, she'd ring the little bell.

"No, that's wrong," she'd say, pouring me another Wild Turkey in a lovely crystal snifter. Right or wrong, it always ended the same way: on the rug, where we'd make passionate love.

The Painter's Wife

I have no idea what her name was. I never even asked. I saw her in a traffic jam and ten minutes later we were in the back of my ever-present truck, just ravishing each other. I never saw her again and realized what I had been doing was a cover, and I needed to stop.

Rosie

But then there was Rosie. I met her on the beach. It was after I realized my pursuits were shallow, unproductive, not lasting, and preventing me from having the committed, intimate relationship I really craved but probably was afraid of. I had made a promise to myself that I was going to stop my fatuous chases and turn over a new leaf. Then I saw Rosie, this beautiful redhead, as we both went out for a swim. She gave me a coy, Ipana toothpaste smile as we emerged from the waves.

But remember: New leaf. Turning over. And she had two little ones with her. I went back to my mat and took a nap on the sand. There I was, at Malibu Beach, exercising uncharacteristic control. I was proud of myself.

But upon awakening, I realized Miss Ipana had moved closer as I slept. She was about fifteen feet away and was calling to me, holding up a magazine.

"What do you think of this?" she asked.

I crawled through the hot sand to her blanket, where she handed me a copy of *Redbook* magazine, open to an article about husbands and premature ejaculation. My new lifestyle immediately went out the window. She had vivid freckles and pendulous breasts. So much for the new leaf.

"You know about this?"

"Well, yeah. It's a common sadness. From what I understand. Which I, of course, personally don't."

"I don't know what I am going to do," she said, and confessed her problem, which was hurting her marriage. Her husband was a hedge fund manager and retired athlete.

"My Teddy is an Adonis," she said. "He's great in the sack. But I don't have enough sex and I'm really horny."

"Oh, Rosie, that's awful," I said. That familiar twinge in my back was occurring again. I looked into her limpid brown eyes. "Rosie, you can remedy that."

"How, Johnny?"

"Well, Rosie," I said, looking into her beautiful brown eyes with sympathetic concern, "you should have an affair."

She'd already considered it, she told me, but thought it would be too complicated. Besides, her husband had a violent temper. Perfect.

"Besides, I know all of Teddy's friends," she said.

Desperate to help this poor, neglected woman, I deeply considered the situation for about three seconds. Then, I offered her a solution.

"Well, Rosie, you don't know me," I said, offering myself selflessly.

"I don't." She smiled.

The little pain in my back was getting worse.

"Rosie, let's go in the ocean," I said seriously.

"What?"

"Let's. Go. In. The. Ocean."

She blushed.

"Oh, I get ya," she said. She was a really smart girl.

She sent her little ones away to get ice cream while I feigned looking for sand crabs on all fours while crawling into the water to conceal myself and my growing ardor. In the waves, I was covered, and she met me there in the foamy Pacific. We held each other in the tide like two swimmers frolicking in the surf. It wasn't easy. I lost traction, as the ocean was a bit rough, but I gave it my best. Big breath, push up from the bottom, thrust, big breath, push up from the bottom, thrust. Finally, the grand finale. And just in time, as the water was getting deeper. I looked at her.

"Are you crying?" I said.

"No," she said, laughing and pointing at the beach. Hundreds of onlookers were gathered at the shoreline, watching us as we were dragged out to sea. At the time, I didn't know what a riptide was. Then two lifeguards with orange paddleboards were coming for us. I waved them off.

"It's okay, guys, I've got her."

But they put us in a harness and towed us to shore. We made the Santa Monica paper the next day: UNIDENTIFIED ACTOR HELPS SAVE DROWNING WOMAN. Even then, I couldn't get a mention.

It's important to remember, if you are ever caught in a riptide, don't swim against it. Swim parallel to the shore until you're out of it. This is, of course, much easier to do when you are uncoupled.

I realize now that most of the pain I felt over the years was from those I loved, and fearing the loss of that love, I always left first—prematurely in many cases, and to my own detriment—or never committed at all. I felt the need to protect myself and would never give anyone the power to hurt me again. My dalliances were enjoyable, because going from one inconsequential relationship to another was safe. But when they were over, I was alone, and the cycle began again. Luckily, physically intimate encounters weren't the only things I had to rely on when times got hard.

People Are Paying Attention
to Whether You're
Paying Attention

ouse, how would you like to be Judy's date tonight at dinner?" Peter Feibleman asked one afternoon. Peter was a gifted writer, and we met at a dinner party hosted by some new friends of mine. He'd written a popular book as well as some great scripts, and after we became friendly he volunteered to introduce me to a few of his producer and director friends in the hope of finding me a new job. He called me Mouse, a term of affection for him, but I don't know where it came from or how he had gotten on it. At the time, Feibleman was dating Buddy Schwab, the famed Broadway dancer and choreographer, and they were a kind of power couple among the so-called gay mafia that had a grip on theater and musicals.

Judy was Judy Garland. Yes, that Judy Garland. I loved everything about her. Not only was she beautiful, but there was such tenderness and passion when she sang. Even now, when I hear

"Over the Rainbow," it still touches me deeply. So when Peter asked me to be Judy's dinner date, I was thrilled.

Peter and Buddy kept a little bungalow in Boys Town, located in West Hollywood. I came early, not wanting to be late for Ms. Garland. The bungalow was renovated and chic. A beautiful table had been set in her honor, the plates and candles and silverware placed just so.

And then Judy came in, floating in a long black dress. She sat next to me and spent the rest of the night sharing some of her most personal stories. We connected, enjoyed each other's company. I felt very close to her, as though we were old friends. She told me how, as a child actress appearing in *The Wizard of Oz*, she would suffer abuse at the hands of the studio executives, who passed her around like chattel. Later on, she confessed that she and other actors were frequently drugged up. The hours on set were so long, the studios would provide pills to keep them awake. They were so wired, she and Mickey Rooney needed other drugs to go to sleep. And then more drugs to wake up again, the cycle continuing. These studio executives she described, the founders of the film business in Hollywood, were all but plantation masters who treated the actors like slaves.

She enthralled us with her insider's tales. One of my favorites says a lot about this gracious woman. It was about Mr. Wonderful, another famous actor.

"I had such a crush on this world-famous lothario," she told me, relating a tale of woeful disappointment.

"One day, he invited me to come out to his home," she said. She had planned all week for the big event, buying a new peignoir, then waiting in suspense after his chauffeur arrived to pick her up and drive her back to his home in the Malibu Colony, the prized beachfront strip home to so many of the stars and Hollywood elite.

The dining room was set when she arrived, the champagne glasses filled and caviar passed. After dinner, like clockwork, the butler and server disappeared. Her young heart was throbbing. And just like in the scripts for the movies they made, Mr. Wonderful got up from the table, picked her up in his arms, and carried her up the elegant staircase to the master bedroom.

The view was magnificent. Through the windows, she could see the waves of the Pacific. It was liquid moonlight, a divine setting.

She watched Mr. Wonderful retreat into the bathroom to prepare for their night of passion. In his absence, alone in the boudoir, she waited, anticipating a night of ecstasy.

"I got undressed," she said, "and slipping on my new peignoir and sliding under the bedsheets, I waited for Mr. Wonderful to emerge.

"I was waiting and waiting, wondering where my Prince Charming had gone."

She grew restless. She got out from under the sheets, walked over to the bathroom, and opened the door. Inside, she looked around. It was empty.

Then she noticed the closet door. She pushed it open, and there he was, bending down on the floor, under the rows of perfectly pressed suits on matching hangers.

"He was putting shoe trees in his slippers."

She left the closet, put all her clothes back on, sprinted downstairs, and begged the chauffeur to take her home. It was a moving story for me. What kind of man carries Judy Garland up the stairs in his arms, has her waiting for him in his bed, and then proceeds to disappear into his closet and put shoe trees inside his slippers? It was always a warning to me. No matter what: Be kind. Be considerate. I always tried to be.

Between Good Friends, "Call Me Anytime" Means Just That

C ookie, life is like a bowl of roses. Just watch out for the pricks," she told me. I had been cast in a two-part episode of *Cannon* called "The Star," and they got one of the biggest to play that role: Joan Fontaine.

I played a rapist and, of course, the killer. Another bad guy. We hit it off immediately. We spent so much time together on set she developed her own nickname for me: "Cookie."

And she was Joni.

They didn't use stand-ins. I had a knife to her throat and was dragging her from room to room in almost every scene. We had a lot of time in between takes while they set up the shots, and we talked and talked. She had been a companion to George Sanders, an ultimate bon vivant, a gentleman's gentleman. He was a sophisticate, upscale, and a good actor who sadly committed suicide.

His note simply read: "Is that all there is?"

Joni had been left without him but still had many friends. I felt so flattered that she included me and that she shared so many marvelous and intimate stories about old Hollywood. One day during shooting, I made a confession. It was my birthday.

"You know, if people could see me, holding one of the most beautiful women in the world in my arms, I would be the envy of everybody. Especially since it's my birthday."

"Cookie, is it your birthday?" she purred in my ear.

"Yes, Joni," I purred back.

"Well, happy birthday, Cookie," she told me, and reached over and gave me a sweet little goose.

"Thanks, Joni," I said, thinking it a lovely gesture.

"*Mais certainemant*, Cookie," she said.

Later that afternoon, I was walking off the Goldwyn lot, dressed casually, to say the least. I had on flip-flops, torn jeans, and a ripped Stanley Kowalski T-shirt. I was heading back to the sailboat I called home when a pea green Rolls-Royce pulled up alongside me. The tinted window went down and that incredible voice came out of the shadows.

"Cookie, do you like caviar?"

I'd never had caviar, not even the smallest of tastes.

"Crazy about it," I said.

"Cookie, do you like champagne?"

"*Mais certainement*," I said, mimicking her sophistication.

"Well, Cookie, why don't you call the wifey and tell her you'll be late? Why don't we go to my digs at the Beverly Hills Hotel?"

My God. Could this be happening? Was this gracious woman actually interested in me? She opened the door to her Rolls-Royce, and I could smell the Parisian perfume. I hopped in, and we wound through the jasmine-scented twilight of Beverly Hills. When we arrived, she opened the door to her spacious hotel suite, with huge bouquets of magnificent flowers throughout and, indeed, the finest of French champagnes. For me, it was not only the beginning of a lifelong love affair with caviar but, more important, a friendship with a very special woman. We talked and talked until the champagne disappeared; then we went down to the Polo Lounge to the table reserved for special stars.

No, Joni wasn't interested in me. Not physically, anyway. But it didn't matter. We shared many personal stories and intimate details. No move was made, and I was fine with that. We liked each other, immensely. It was a magnificent night. I felt awfully good.

"Cookie, do you ever get to New York?" she said.

"Oh, sure," I said, which was not exactly the truth.

Since leaving home, I'd never made an effort to go back. My father would come each winter to escape the snow, as would Uncle Herbie, whenever he could get a free ride on a gambling junket to Vegas.

"Take my number," she said. "I'd love to see you again, and please don't hesitate to call under any circumstances. Do you understand me, Cookie?"

"Sure, Joni."

As it happened, about ten years later, I found myself in New York and in need of a friend. I'd been cast for a part on a stupid soap opera called *Days of Our Lives,* playing a deprogrammer. They had flown me out from Los Angeles, which made me feel very good. I had endless boring dialogue and got it straight twenty times, but the so-called star kept blowing it. It was New

Year's Eve when it came time for the twenty-first take or so, and it was my turn to blow it.

They went into overtime and golden time. Guess who got fired? On the spot. Suddenly I was in the familiar position of having no money and no job. I walked around Broadway on the fringe of the huge crowds. It was a cold night and I had no place to go, no place to stay. What was I going to do? What would I tell my father? I was due at his farm the next day.

Then it occurred to me. I flipped through my little black book and dialed her number. The phone rang twice, three times, and she picked up.

"Ms. Fontaine," I said, "you probably don't remember—"

"Cookie, darling. Is that you?"

"Yeah, Joni."

"What are you doing? Where are you?"

"I'm in New York and I'm not doing anything. I just lost a job—"

"Cookie, you get in a taxi right now and come over to my apartment. I'm having a party for some people who can't wait to meet you."

I hailed a taxi and soon found myself at the foot of a swanky building on the Upper East Side. The doorman in his cap and gloves waved me into a mahogany-paneled elevator. Up I went, the door opened, and there was Joan Fontaine in an elegant gray gown, a pearl choker around her neck, hair up in a chignon, as glamorous as ever.

"I'm so glad to see you, Cookie," she said, hugging me, taking me by the arm, and introducing me to her socialite guests as "my dear friend from Hollywood." The night went on, the New Year's ball dropped, and I was the last guest. I had nowhere to go.

"Cookie, do you need a place to stay?" she asked.

"No, I'm fine," I said.

"Well, you must let me make you breakfast."

She went and changed into her pajamas, and we sat in her kitchen as the sun came up. She made me scrambled eggs and the best croissants I ever had. Our conversation was like an interrupted sentence from so many years before. We talked of many things, of lost love, of friendship, and of survival in the industry. I still had a lot to prove. I am sure she never knew how important she was to me. This sophisticated, world-renowned star chose me, an often-out-of-work actor, to be her friend.

The lines we draw between us—lines of class, lines of wealth, lines of success or failure—are not real but drawn by us. I will forever be humbled and flattered that Joni looked at me and, for whatever reason, chose to draw her own conclusions instead. Her caring and kindness will never be forgotten.

Act III

I saw 200 South La Brea, the massive glassy casting studio where they were holding auditions for the Dos Equis beer commercial. Parking was always tricky in Hollywood, and I found a spot down the block. I asked a nice shopkeeper to please put in the quarters I gave him once an hour had passed. It was a main thoroughfare. With the day I was having, I could end up with a very expensive traffic ticket. With my luck, my trusty Ford with my bed in the back—what felt like my current home—would get towed. Then I would really be a hobo. I would have nothing at all. Even Skid Row was a long way from Hollywood. I thought about leaving and going anywhere else instead. Why was I wasting my time?

When I crossed the street and arrived at the building, I couldn't believe the size of the crowd milling outside. It was ridiculous—the line of actors was backed up around the block. I couldn't tell how many were waiting—perhaps four hundred, five hundred. Too many people, too much competition, and the wait could take forever. Time to go, I thought.

I doubled back for the truck and heard my agent Barbara's voice in my head: "You what? You left without even trying? What if they would have picked you? You never know if you don't try. Just give it your best shot and forget about it."

She was right. Or at least that voice in my head was right. I doubled back again to the building, sat down, and scanned the competition. This audition made no sense for me. All the actors around me were far younger—and Latino. Which did make sense. Dos Equis is a Mexican beer. Naturally, the advertising agency and production company would want a Latino to play the lead. Now I was starting to get angry. What was Barbara thinking? Should I get a new agent? I thought about calling her from the phone in the lobby and telling her, This isn't worth the time. I'm wrong. They're looking for a Latino. All these guys look like they are going out to play Juan Valdez, the coffee guy. I'm a Jewish guy from the Bronx.

But for a Jewish guy from the Bronx, I'd certainly had some far-flung experiences.

Everyone Needs to Be Haunted
Once in Their Life

B ack then, I spent a lot of time driving up to the old gold-rush towns and trout streams of California, places like Lone Pine and Aberdeen, which lured so many miners with their picks and pans, all pining for gold and the promise of found fortune and leaving their lost dreams behind to decay with the frames of old buildings and forgotten locales.

I'd come here for the fly-fishing, some of the best in the country outside of Montana. Many of my most memorable days were spent on Virginia Creek, a stream that runs through pasture-land and the high prairies, cattle ranches, and rolling foothills of the Sierra Nevada. This was Ansel Adams country, and I spent many a day wading in Cottonwood Creek, down near Lone Pine. I once shot a rattlesnake à la Roy Rogers. Another time, I pulled out a golden trout at eight thousand feet. I still remember holding this rare marvel of nature in my hands, the fish shining with iridescent gold and purple and red. And then there was

Mono Lake, whose waters were so salty that the only forms of life below the surface were prehistoric creatures like brine shrimp and alkali flies.

I had dropped off my Parisian girlfriend at the bus station prematurely, after she spent her first and last night in a tent. ("My zizi is frozen," she said after waking up.) With my ice chest already loaded with trout, I figured it would make sense to skip fishing that afternoon and check out Bodie, a legendary ghost town. The road itself was a hellish thirteen miles out on Highway 395. It was a crisp day late in fall, and the road was already a mess of mud and frozen ground.

From a distance, I could see the remnants of the town, the frames and structures leaning into one another. Through the windshield, I read the welcome sign.

UNLAWFUL TO TAKE ANYTHING FROM BODIE, it read.

The sign was a municipal one, but it also was a nod to the Curse of Bodie.

Bodie was late to the gold rush. After the first strike in 1848, at Sutter's Mill, which was farther north, on the way to Sacramento, miners like the town's founder, W. S. Bodie, believed they were on their way to find the mother lode of discoveries that would make them rich. Bodie never lived to see his town evolve, however. During a blizzard, he ventured off in the snow to fetch supplies from a neighboring town and disappeared. The following spring, he was discovered in the thawing snow with a broken leg. He hadn't survived, but his town had. In the 1870s, an accidental explosion in a mine uncovered a major vein of gold. Within days of the discovery, miners began to flood in from around the world. Bodie grew so fast that folks in the area joked it was the third-largest city in California, which wasn't true, though the town was big enough to host hundreds of saloons, brothels, a racetrack, a Chinatown, and plenty of criminals. Bodie was so dangerous that one local story has a young girl kneeling down and praying to the heavens upon learning her family was moving there. "Good-bye, God!" she cried, her hands clasped.

Like many boomtowns, Bodie didn't last long. The town was prosperous for a few decades, but after a few fires, there wasn't much left. Instead of packing up their belongings, the townspeople simply left hurriedly when news of the next "strike" occurred, taking with them only what they could carry in their covered wagons, leaving the rest of their possessions behind in the buildings that remained. The structures were thus filled with rough-hewn furniture, antiques, utensils, and tools. The historic curios made for compelling souvenirs, but it was a widespread belief that anyone who swiped an object from the town would suffer bad luck and be connected to the ghosts of the town. These spirits were often seen through the dark windows, turning on lights where no electric lines supported them. The music of the day was reported in buildings that had been uninhabited and crumbling for decades.

Tourists come to witness the abandoned place but were long gone this late in the season. I was curious about the reports of these spirits and drove into town, thankful to put those thirteen miles of hell behind me. I now found myself on a high plateau that was about as busy as the moon. Bodie was creepy, eerie. The windows in the buildings were dark, and even though nobody was around I had the unquestionable feeling that I was being watched.

I thought about turning around and leaving—no good could come, I figured, from lingering here—and then I noticed that a truck was parked down the street. Driving closer, I found that the truck was stamped with an official seal: US PARK RANGER. Looking down the street, I saw a figure carrying something and disappearing into the back of a house. The structure was sound, and a few tended flowers in a box outside were holding their own, challenging the coming winter. Somebody was living here.

I knocked on the door.

"Come on in."

I opened the door and saw a park ranger. He introduced himself as Cal Rogers, and after an amiable back-and-forth, he told me of a problem he was having.

A varmint hunter had passed through the day before, he said. As he was leaving the town in his truck, the hunter's pair of coonhounds had jumped out the window, perhaps to chase something. The hunter never came back to get them, and the coonhounds were missing.

"Don't blame 'em," Rogers said. "That guy was kind of a prick."

All day, Rogers said, he'd been out searching the town and the prairies, using a fresh piece of meat as bait to get the coonhounds to emerge from their hiding place. In the morning, he'd captured the female, he said, and pointed inside, where she was now snoring away by the fire.

"The other poor guy is still out there," he said, and, given the drop in temperature and falling sun in the late afternoon, he was worried. The land around Bodie was lonely, barren, and filled with coyotes, he said. A mountain lion had also been spotted nearby, and with the night falling, predators would be out, he was nervous the missing coonhound would not survive another night.

"Mind helping me find him?" Rogers said.

Great, I thought. Another mountain rescue mission.

"Sure," I said, and we split up to cover more ground. Rogers walked back through the main street, and I walked up and out of town and onto a bluff. Rogers had also given me a piece of meat to use as bait, and I walked with it high in the air, hoping the wind would blow its scent in whatever direction the missing coonhound had been hiding. About an hour passed, and I heard him crying.

I looked around, unable to locate the dog. Then I spotted him hiding under a large rock. He was snarling, untrusting, hungry. I walked closer to him, the meat extended.

He bared his fangs. This was not going to be easy.

I found a nearby rock and sat down, showing the dog I was not approaching him and meant him no harm. I then removed my belt, fashioning the leather strip into a leash, and let the piece of meat do the talking. Eventually, that coonhound crawled out from his hiding spot, made his way toward me, and soon was gobbling up the meat and licking my hands. I dropped the leash over him without any protest and walked him proudly back into town.

"Oh my God!" Rogers said, thanking me profusely. "How the hell did you do that?"

"Thank the meat," I said, and began to head back to my truck. It was now dusk. I had a long drive back to Los Angeles.

"Hey, listen, it's getting late," Rogers said. "How about joining me for dinner? I have some great steaks and a bottle of bourbon."

Hunting for the dog, I'd worked up an appetite. I was cold too, and a sip of whiskey wouldn't hurt.

"Works for me," I said, and returned to his abode. He didn't have a potbelly stove but a sheepherder stove, a simple design shaped like a box. Sheepherder stoves were designed to be portable and featured a flat top.

"I can cook anything and everything on that stove," he said as he sprinkled a handful of salt on top of the stove. He placed another log on the fire, closing the door as the flames grew and the temperature rose. Soon he produced a massive steak. He tossed the meat onto the stove—without a skillet or pan—and the smoke and aroma filled the room. Soon enough, we were sitting to eat.

"This used to be the old brothel," he said as we started to slice our way through the tender steak, easily the best I'd ever had.

The ranger poured out another glass of the bourbon.

"You might as well spend the night," he said. "Too late to go back—looks like an early storm is on its way."

I hadn't heard about the storm, but the High Sierra was notorious for freak squalls, and, according to Rogers, the area was one of the coldest places in America. It was so desolate and such a target for snow that the sheriff's department had to air-drop him food and supplies to survive the winter. The town had no phone lines either. Rogers's only way to contact them—or anyone in the outside world, for that matter—was a shortwave radio.

I took him up on his offer and spent the night in the old brothel. The wallpaper was peeling off the walls behind the red leather banquettes. The furniture was original. Like everything else in the town, the place had hardly been touched, except for Rogers's small additions to make it livable. It was like stepping back in time.

I asked him about the ghosts.

"We don't see them all that often, actually," he said.

"Is the curse real?" I asked Rogers.

"Real as you are here," he said, and explained that the old saloons and bawdy houses, still adorned with objects from a century or more before, were also the homes of ghosts. Park rangers over the years who'd spent time in Bodie claimed to have experienced strange behaviors, he said, and few lasted more than a season. Loneliness took its toll, and rumor had it that one ranger who braved the winter in Bodie took his own life. Suicides were not unusual here in its heyday.

There were stories. Like the one about the Cain House, named after James Cain, a businessman who made a fortune hauling lumber into Bodie to build the mines. Mr. Cain had a Chinese maid, and they had a torrid affair, or so the tale went, and after rumors began to spread through Bodie, he fired her. But instead of leaving the home, the woman committed suicide in the upstairs bedroom. In that very room, strange sightings were reported: bedroom lights flashing on and off, even a feeling of suffocation by those in the building.

Or the Mendocini House. After a long winter, one park ranger opened the door and smelled the lingering trace of garlic and tomatoes and the remnants of Italian cooking. What had been happening? The sounds of children playing had been heard too, and music, as if a party were under way.

Rogers didn't seem to mind. He had the sensibilities of a poet, or so it seemed.

"Just part of the job," he said.

"You ever get lonely here?" I asked.

"Why do you think I asked you to stay?" Rogers said, and laughed. We effortlessly drained his bottle of bourbon. It was an incredible night, a chance to meet a new friend. I promised to return the next year.

"You bring the bourbon, I'll bring the steaks," he said, solidifying our deal. Leaving the town, I made a vow to keep my promise. Besides, I had to return. I was curious. Did the ghosts of Bodie exist? Was the Curse of Bodie really true?

I was late. The Bodie winter came and went, with the road buried under twenty feet of snow. I returned to the High Sierra only for the opening of the spring trout season. Still, I woke to find six inches of snow on the top of my tent. No sense in fishing. I went to the sheriff's station in nearby Bridgeport and asked about Cal Rogers. Had he emerged from Bodie yet? I figured the snow must have kept him in for the past five months.

"He's making his first trip out today," the sheriff said. "He's on his way into town now."

"Can you radio him for me?" I asked, and soon I could hear the crackling of Rogers's voice on the other end of the line.

"How would you like to come back to town?" he said.

"Love to." I was out of work anyway. As usual.

"You got chains for your tires?" he asked.

"Of course. And a four-wheel-drive truck."

"Well, wait for me there at the sheriff's station," he said. "We'll drive up together."

The day had turned cold and miserable. I went to fetch a bottle of bourbon in town (and a reserve for Rogers, just in case), and when I returned he was waiting in his truck. It was getting late, and after a quick hello I got back into my truck and followed him up the so-called road.

It had become like a tunnel of snow, the banks of ice alongside glistening and rising some twenty feet. On the high prairie there was nothing to block the wind, and it shrieked around the mountain, creating monstrous snowdrifts. Always the wind, blowing without end. Looking up, I was reminded of El Greco's *View of Toledo*, one of my favorite paintings, the swirling gray clouds obscuring the leaden sky.

We were closing in on Bodie when I saw the brake lights of Rogers's truck. He'd stopped. Had he hit something? A malfunction? He got out of his truck and walked back to me. He looked deep in thought, as if he were mulling something over.

I rolled down the window. He leaned in.

"I have a visitor," he said.

That wasn't a problem for me.

"I just want to tell you, or to kind of forewarn you . . ." And then he told me about his daughter. "She's recovering from an accident. It was horrible, and she's got scars. Bad ones. All the scar tissue is on one side of her face. She's been with me now all winter, just laying low and recovering until she heals enough to have her next operation and return to civilization.

"I just didn't want you to get surprised," he said, and returned to his truck. Half an hour later, I was back in Bodie, which had been buried under several layers of heavy, deep snow all winter and was just beginning to thaw out. I followed Rogers into the old cathouse with my pack and gear. That's when I saw her, waiting near the staircase.

Grace was beautiful. Rogers's daughter was tall and slender. She had long hair the color of winter wheat, not quite blond, light freckles on her face, and full lips. Her eyes were lonely, perhaps more gray than blue.

I walked over to greet her and stopped abruptly. Now that I was closer, I could see the damage on one side of her face. It was nasty. There was no other way to describe it.

The injuries were brutal, and no doubt permanent. I did my best not to react. I admired her stoic demeanor, though she looked forlorn. I also felt pity for her, saddened that something so ugly could happen by accident to someone so soft and pretty.

"A car accident," she said. Nothing more; then she disappeared up the stairs.

It was dark now, and Rogers tossed the logs into the sheepherder stove like last time, then tossed a steak on the stove. Again, the whorehouse was filled with a wonderful smell now familiar to me, and I heard footsteps on the stairs. Grace had returned for dinner.

We sat around the table and I don't remember what we talked about. She was proud and comfortable enough not to hide. I couldn't help but admire Grace's beauty. I was careful not to look too closely, for obvious reasons. Other than her father and the surgeon, she probably hadn't seen another man in six months.

Rogers poured me a glass of bourbon and looked out the window. The snow had started, and through the flurries I imagined the horse-drawn wagons of miners and settlers passing through Bodie, illuminated only by the flicker of gas lanterns. Closing my eyes, I was sure I could hear the sounds of a saloon organ playing a rag and the bickering of drunk miners at the bar, threatening to punch each other's rotten teeth out or pull their pistols. We drank some more, and when I tried to look out again, the windows were covered in windblown snow.

Rogers got up and excused himself for the night. Now Grace and I were alone. The conversation continued.

Grace was interesting. She told me that in her spare time she'd walk down to the library in Bodie, which, like everything else, was abandoned, and read through the old books and gaze at the maps and other artifacts that were left behind in the 1870s.

She was even writing her own book, she said.

"About what?" I asked.

She wouldn't say.

The wood stove needed another log. I reached over to the pile and stuffed the stove with logs, dampening the fire to keep the heat up through the night. I stood up to retreat to the guest room at the top of the stairs. Grace looked at me questioningly. Inside, after closing the door, I walked around the guest room, pacing the floorboards. It was odd, how conveniently Rogers had extricated himself from the table. Was I a gift to his daughter? Would she be joining me? Outside, I could hear the creaking from the ghost town's swinging doors and broken windows at the mercy of the night wind. I got into the bed, under the quilt and flannel sheets, thinking about Grace.

Then the bedroom door slowly opened.

In the sliver of light from the cracked door, I could see that Grace had changed into her nightgown. She stood in the doorway. Without saying a word, she walked to the bed and slipped in beside me. I could feel her bare feet against mine. Her skin was warm and soon I could feel all of her against me. I kissed her on the forehead. I pulled her closer and held her tight for a long time, just embracing her lovingly.

That night, Grace told me the truth. There had never been a car accident. It was her cover story. She had been cut up with a knife at the hands of an old boyfriend. His name was Reno. He was a hit man, a contract murderer, a detail she learned only after she met him. She never told me why he took a knife to her cheek. Maybe it's just as well. Months after the attack, she was terrified. Reno was to go to trial soon for some of the many charges against him. Prosecutors were looking for witnesses. She would be subpoenaed. Reno could chase her down, even in Bodie. She worried that she might never escape him.

I positioned her head on my shoulder in the bed, stroking her hair softly, slowly easing her to sleep. I closed my eyes, listening to the howl of the old windows rattling in the snowstorm, thinking about the ghosts in the houses down Main Street, the moans of old miners, thinking about Reno. What kind of name was Reno? It was like the name of an old miner who had come to this brothel a hundred years ago, looking for gold. Who cuts up a girl like Grace with a knife? And what in the hell was I doing here? Was all this really happening? The drama felt more like it belonged in the gold-rush days of Bodie. Was Reno really a reincarnated ghost of an old thug in this town? Was Grace the same, maybe the spirit of an old brothel girl, a vestige of another time and place whom I now had wrapped up in my arms? If they were ghosts why could I see them? Had I become a ghost too, in returning to Bodie? Or were my mind and the bourbon playing a devious trick on me at this altitude and in the bedroom of the old cathouse?

I reached out to touch her again. Was she real? She turned to me and I could feel her warmth and breathing against my chest. I caressed her face and placed a kiss on her damaged cheek. As I did, a tear crawled its way to me. I still remember its taste.

W aking up, I hadn't expected to find her beside me. Surely Grace was an invention of my mind, the result of too much drink and the ghost town winds. But she was there, huddled under the flannel sheets. I slipped out of the bed, went downstairs, and looked for Rogers. His ranger truck was gone. I looked outside. The sun was out and the snow was dazzling.

"Want to see the library?" Grace asked, inching down the stairs in bare feet.

"Sure."

"We can use the snowshoes," she said, and after getting ready we laced up the pairs she and her father kept by the door. I grabbed my camera from my pack and followed her out the front door into the sunny fields and snow.

I had trouble keeping up with Grace. She was different today, light and wound up with energy. She knew every building, every backstory. We went into the schoolhouse, the courthouse, then finally the Bodie Library, her favorite place. We looked around, flipping through the pages and maps that the miners had left behind.

Scanning the old books and local histories, I saw a familiar collection of works by one of my favorite authors. It was a large volume of William Shakespeare's plays, bound and printed in another era. I ran my finger along the weathered spine. *A Midsummer Night's Dream* was my favorite. I had performed scenes from it in class as a young actor.

> *Love looks not with the eyes, but with the mind;*
> *And therefore is wing'd Cupid painted blind.*
> *Nor hath Love's mind of any judgement taste—*
> *Wings and no eyes figure unheedy haste.*

I was delighted to stumble on such a treasure. In this dead library, such gold was a waste.

"Could I keep this?" I said, forgetting all about the Curse of Bodie and the history of bad things that had befallen those who removed objects from the ghost town.

"Sure," she said, and led us back out into the snow, now familiar to me. We kept moving down the main street where the old Chinatown must have been, and down past the site of the old racetrack, perhaps impossible to imagine in the dunes of snow that covered the town. We kept on going in our snowshoes, leaving tracks to the outskirts of the town. I reached into my jacket pocket for my camera to take a picture of the old town. From here, we could see Bodie as it was in the late 1870s, as the miners flooded into this boomtown of sin and fast money. I removed one of my snowshoes and held it up, angling the camera lens through the webbing and leather straps. Adjusting the exposure, I snapped a few images, never wanting to forget this moment and specialness I came to feel for Grace.

We all had dinner again, eating around the wood stove like a family. Soon the bourbon was gone and so was Rogers, retiring to his quarters. The snow had stopped, and through the windows of the brothel the town and valley were cast in a soft, surreal haze.

"How would you like to snowshoe through the town under a full moon?" Grace asked.

"Let's go." And we were off again into the old town, watching our reflections in the windows of old saloons and brothels, so delighted to enjoy the isolation of the abandoned town, not a soul to distract us from each other.

I'll always remember the last night we spent together in Bodie, holding her as she slept, knowing it would be the last time I would see her. Relationships that bloom under special conditions like those are never perennial. When you try to put them back together, the pieces never fit the second time around. At a different location, the feelings falter and disappear. In the morning, I kissed her on the forehead and disappeared down the stairs.

Sitting near the stove in the old brothel, Rogers was waiting for me with a steaming cup of coffee. It was time to go. There was nothing more to say. He walked me to my truck in silence and waited until I climbed up into the driver's seat.

"See you next year?" he said.

"I'll get the bourbon," I said. But we both knew it might not happen. I felt like I had been in Bodie forever. Maybe I had.

. . .

In my library, on a far corner of a shelf, next to a few old fishing books my father gave me and several works of poetry written by friends, I still have the collection of Shakespeare's works that I took with me from Bodie, bound up like an old volume of the Talmud. I can't say that strange things happened or misfortune befell me after I left the town with my stolen book. But I carry a certain sweet pain of the wonderful closeness I shared with a stranger and the sorrow of never seeing her again. I was cursed by Bodie, indeed.

Not All Good Guys
Are Good

I've always been fascinated by the applications of folk medicine in the modern world, and I have had the good fortune to befriend a number of shamans, who not only have taught me their own versions of witchcraft but have opened me up to understanding powers and wisdom at the core of natural healing. It is not the body. It is the mind.

I heard tales of healing from my grandfather Alexander, who lived with the Navajo during the Great Depression and learned their methods of healing. In college, I read *Man's Unconquerable Mind,* in which author Gilbert Highet talks about how we use only a small percentage of our mental powers. He illustrated under hypnosis the incredible feats we can accomplish. Years later, I studied hypnosis myself and learned how much one can expand the potential of mental possibility. I was mesmerized by the feats of the believers, the swamis, the monks, and the holy men who were capable of lowering their body temperature, heart and respiration rates and enduring extremes of cold with no adverse effects.

My father also taught me about the powers of the mind. He once told me a story about a guy who had a terrible fear of snakes. He was bitten by a snake one day, and he was convinced that he was going to die. And he did. Later, they found out the bite was from a garter snake. Just a common snake—wasn't even venomous. But the guy died anyway. Scared himself to death.

And then, of course, there was One-Eyed Betty, with her voodoo. It didn't work for me. But it must have for her, because she kept doing it long after I left home.

I met Dr. Benji in Manila, on my first trip to the Philippines. I was shooting a film called *Green Eyes*. One minute we were in the jungle, so primitive it was as if we'd stepped back in time. The next moment, we'd be at a strip mall, surrounded by hypermodern billboards. Many of them advertised the mysterious practice of psychic surgery. We saw it advertised between television shows too.

Apparently, these Filipino "doctors" had the magic power to open up the body cavity and excise diseased tissue with only their minds. They were mentalists, performing these heavy-duty operations with smoldering herb-infused cotton and energetic incantations from the Bible. It was a phenomenon, and airplane loads of tourists were flying into Manila from around the world to see these famous psychic surgeons, one of which was Dr. Benji.

I was staying at the Conrad Manila, which was located in the southern part of the city, right across the street from Barrio Fiesta. I needed only a few minutes, perhaps less, to fall in love with the raw chaos and primal charms of Manila. The sounds of the city were unlike anything you could hear in an American city, a place that felt alive and vibrant and tuned in. In the morning, I woke to the lyrical sounds of the muezzin chanting through a tinny loud-speaker and watched the Filipinos doing their daily tai chi in the park, practicing that balletic exercise of focus, routine, and rhythm.

The noise was constant. The cacophony of traffic and confusion was a symphony of cheap car horns, zipping motor scooters, and the engines of jeepneys, the American jeeps that had been left on the island after World War II and had become works of art. The Filipinos painted them over in colors of bright orange, hot pink, and parrot green. I felt so at ease, devouring the *lumpia,* which is a Filipino egg roll, and the crispy *pata,* or fatty pork fried up with flour. The food was magnificent, the beer was cold, and the women were everywhere and flirtatious, coy, charming, demure, and just adoring of men.

The filming was nonstop. We shot every day in the jungle at a place where they were building the set at Pangasinan falls for *Apocalypse Now,* as well as at different locations throughout the city. One night, we were doing an all-night shoot in Manila proper. The location was the American embassy, and the producers had gone around the city to wrangle up Caucasians so we could have enough extras in the scene to duplicate an accurate formal affair.

I had a leading part. Before we started shooting, I met the extra who was to play my girlfriend. Her name was Nancy Price. She was from Las Vegas, an attractive blonde, and we filmed and shot throughout the night as boyfriend and girl-friend. Maybe the artificial intimacy led to real feelings, or perhaps the romance of foreigners living in an exotic place like Manila made it easy to enjoy a quick rapport.

I was curious about how Nancy wound up in Manila.

"I'm studying reflexology," she told me. "My father is a reflexologist in LA. And I'm actually here studying with one of the leading psychic surgeons."

That was all I had to hear. I now had a connection into psychic surgery, and I started to pepper Nancy with questions. How did it all work?

"Oh, it's very real," she said, explaining that there were no knives. Just the power of prayer and concentration.

I had no reason to doubt her. Nancy was intelligent and articulate. She was here as a practicing professional. I wanted to believe her. I wanted to be healed too. I'd had stomach problems since my arrivals in the Phillipines and asked her if I could witness one of the surgeries.

"Let me see what I can do," she said.

We shot all night. The next day I was supposed to visit Tokyo after getting a few hours of sleep. But as I got into bed, the phone rang. It was Nancy.

"Dr. Benji is coming to my compound," she said. "Would you like to come and witness?"

I got out of bed, anxious to see firsthand the much-touted doctor. I hopped in a taxi and headed for the compound. At the time, Manila was under a state of martial law, and armed guards with submachine guns and less-than-friendly stares were everywhere. It was a chaotic time in the Philippines.

When the taxi arrived, I got my first look at Nancy's compound, which resembled a military fort. Standing post outside was a guard—armed, of course. Nearby were sandbags piled on top of one another, and other guards walked the perimeter clutching automatic weapons.

I was expected. One of the guards escorted me inside. It was a two-story compound, chickens and all. The climate was scorchingly hot and nothing was insulated; most people couldn't afford air conditioners. The hum of overhead fans was everywhere. The place was upscale jungle: bamboo, reeds, palm fronds, batik, some carved wood objects. As Nancy walked me upstairs to her room, I noticed that she looked even better than she had the long night before.

"Would you like some tea?" she said.

"Yes, I would. Thanks very much."

She sent her houseboy to fetch it—it seemed like all but the poor had their own houseboys. They were available for very little money. Many were excellent cooks and nannies as well. Male or female, there was no difference, and sometimes it was hard to tell which was which.

Her man poured the hot tea. I held the delicate porcelain cup and started to sip: it was aromatic and delicious, with a taste I couldn't quite identify.

"Dr. Benji should be here in a few hours," she said. "When he arrives, I'll ask him if you can witness the surgery."

"Great," I said. "Thanks so much for this, Nancy. Really."

I was drowsy. Nancy was looking better and better.

"Would you like a treatment?" she asked. Sounded just fine to me.

"Sure," I said, and began to remove my clothes down to my underwear. There was no table, so I lay facedown on the only bed in the room: hers. She straddled me, and I could feel the softness of her breasts graze my head. I enjoyed her considerable skill. I told her I would like to return the favor. I always felt an obligation to give back. Her magic continued, as did my fantasies, but I was starting to fall asleep. What a wonderful way to remember Manila, which I was leaving in a few days. I couldn't believe my luck. I was going to score.

But then the compound was overcome with commotion. I could hear the scampering of feet in the hallways, and loud chattering broke my reverie. The honored guest had arrived.

"Dr. Benji's here! Dr. Benji's here!" she said. And she stopped the treatment. So much for my luck.

The door of the room swung open. A small Filipino man in a short-sleeved barong entered the room. He was very slender, with thick glasses. This was the famous Dr. Benji.

I got up from the bed and greeted him. In my underwear.

Nancy told him that I was an American here visiting to make a film and that I was very interested in psychic surgery and the power to heal others.

"He would like to witness," she said.

"Okay, okay," Dr. Benji said. "You witness."

"How did you get this gift?" I asked him.

"When the Japanese occupied my country, we fled to the hills," he said. Without access to medical care, Dr. Benji and others used their abilities to cure diseases and sicknesses.

"Some of us were imbued with this power to heal," he said. "It's a blessing. I've been able to help many people."

I followed them into a larger adjoining room. It was filled with bamboo and pictures of fish. The only piece of furniture was a bed.

The first patient had a serious problem. He was a young Filipino man who had come from the provinces with his parents and had developed a cyst on his neck. The young man lay down on the bed, sweating profusely. He was in pain. He was shaking. His parents were very upset as well.

From the bed, the young man looked up at me.

"I have cancer," he said.

I didn't know what to say.

"I fix," Dr. Benji answered.

"How are you going to fix?" I asked. I looked at the cyst. It was a large, ugly growth that had formed on this poor man's neck.

"I remove," he said simply.

He then looked over at Nancy and sent her to the bathroom. I looked around at the poor parents, who had come here with their sick son. If cancerous, the cyst was potentially fatal. Without complete removal in a proper operating theater, the prognosis was bad.

Then I heard the prayers. It was Nancy. She had come back from the bathroom, chanting passages from a Bible—who knows which one—and holding a smoldering ball of cotton, a little plastic blue bowl, and a blue washcloth. She passed the objects and flaming cotton ball to Dr. Benji, who started wailing to the heavens in Tagalog.

Dr. Benji approached the young man, who was clearly in awe of the whole scene, the smoldering cotton, and the wailing sounds of prayer. Dr. Benji put his hands over the young man and proceeded to perform his "miracles."

"Ah, you have cancer," he said. "I take out. No problem. We fix good."

Dr. Benji turned the young man over on his stomach, and I angled myself to get into a good position to watch his hands and witness the operation. And as I watched his manipulations, all of a sudden, I was looking into what I perceived to be the spine of a human being. Dr. Benji made an opening in what I thought was the body of this young man. I couldn't believe it.

What the hell did Nancy put in that tea? I thought. I was careful not to take my eyes off Dr. Benji, who reached into what appeared to be the body cavity and made some spastic, manipulative movements. As he did this, the cotton ball smoldered. He kept on chanting mumbo jumbo from the Bible. And then he pulled out what looked like a piece of liver with some entrails and a little blood on it. He then dropped it into the little plastic blue bowl that Nancy had brought up. Dr. Benji took the smoldering cotton and rubbed it over what appeared to be an opening in the young man's body while Nancy took the little bowl with the excised tissue and disappeared into the bathroom.

I thought, Oh my God. What did I just see? This is going to change the world! Surely I had been drugged.

I had so many questions for Dr. Benji.

"Where's the blood?" I asked.

"No blood," he answered. "Cauterize from the mind."

"Why is the cyst still there?"

"Only hematoma. Swelling. Will disappear, two, three days."

I smiled in delight. Dr. Benji was a revolutionary shaman. He could change the course of civilization, transforming modern medicine and healing those who could not afford costly surgeries.

He turned to me.

"You have problem?" he asked.

"Yes, since I've been in the Philippines, I have a problem with my stomach," I said. Just like everyone else who visited the Philippines. "I have some discomfort."

"Let me see," he said, placing his hands against my stomach, pushing here and squeezing there.

"I fix," he said.

"Intestine twisted."

"How are you going to fix?"

"I remove."

"You are going to surgically remove?"

"With mind."

I stifled a laugh. Despite what I had seen, the jury was still out for me.

"Dr. Benji, thank you," I said. "I'm going to be in Beverly Hills in two weeks. I'll go to my doctor."

"Okay, but I can fix," he said.

"No, no. But thanks," I said, and inspected the next patient: a man who had a cyst on his cheek. And the next: a young girl with a tumor on her breast. After getting permission from his patients, I watched the procedures. Each performance was similar. The same blue bowl, the same smoldering ball of cotton, the same organ with entrails and blood on it. Wait just a minute. Something was off. How could each bit of excised tissue look the same, from entirely different ailments?

"Nancy, I want that," I said, pointing to the tissue that Dr. Benji had placed in the blue bowl for the third time.

"What?" she said.

"I want that material that he took—that he excised from this girl's breast."

"Why?" she said.

"I want it analyzed."

"I have to ask the doctor," she said.

"Go ahead."

She walked over to Dr. Benji. He said that I could keep the matter and not only have it analyzed but share it with any doctor

I wanted to back in the United States. I believe he thought I was a financial pipeline, as he hinted a few times that I would get a good deal on treatment if I was to share my amazement as to his miracle surgeries back home.

"Just don't let them tell you it's chicken guts," he said.

Don't ask me how, but I got the tissue back to the United States fresh and untainted. In those days, you could fly with anything. I dropped it off at the office of a veterinarian I became friendly with and whose wife, Kay, knew the county medical examiner. She agreed to have the organ tested for me on the sly, and I anxiously waited for the results.

"We got the tests back in," the vet said a few days later.

"What's the verdict?"

"Not of human origin. We're pretty sure it's chicken guts."

Dr. Benji was no miracle worker. But he was as good as any sleight-of-hand expert I had ever seen. The animal parts were arranged in the blue washcloth, placed there surreptitiously by my blond friend. I thought of all those patients who went home to die from what could've been a simple routine operation. That's the simple explanation.

What's harder to explain is the others who had terminal prognoses who had made incredible recoveries from such procedures and went on to lead long and productive lives. Some people pray their ills away. Some go to modern hospitals. Some have Dr. Benji produce chicken guts out of thin air while breathing cotton smoke and listening to Bible readings and Tagalog chants. Was he a charlatan? Or a savior?

Like most of us, I think he was a little of both.

Some Good Guys
Are Just Good

The French Connection was a marvelous film, garnering a number of Academy Awards, including Best Actor for Gene Hackman. He played a cop who closed the largest drug bust of all time in those days, a whopping 112 pounds of heroin. Hackman played the wonder cop credited with this arrest: Popeye Doyle, based on the real-life New York police detective Eddie Egan.

The truth was that it had little to do with great police work. In fact, the bust was actually an accident. How do I know this? Because once he made the bust and became famous, Eddie Egan moved to Hollywood. And that's where we met and became very, very good friends. (He was, in fact, the godfather to my son David.) He was the funniest guy I ever knew.

I met him at Warner Bros. Studios. We were working on different shows. I was walking through the cafeteria on my lunch break and this big hand grabs my wrist.

"I've been looking for you," he said.

I knew who he was. In those days, everyone did. But I had no idea why he was looking for me.

"Let's go for a walk."

He was putting together a film—a continuation of *The French Connection,* how the 112 pounds of dope was stolen from the police locker by crooked cops and sold—yep—right back to the drug dealers. It was a great story.

Eddie wanted me to play his partner, Sonny Grosso, so perfectly embodied by Roy Scheider in *The French Connection.* I couldn't believe my good fortune. Eddie Egan was the real McCoy, and he wanted me. At that moment, he was a hot property, wanted by everyone.

He was also a world-class bullshit artist. A charming one, with a story, to be sure. But a bullshit artist. He had the tale and the way to tell it. He just needed money. For some reason, he wanted my help raising it.

I knew there was a catch.

But hey, who in Hollywood doesn't want to be both an actor and a producer? I took the bait, and we got to work. We set up our first unofficial office at Houlihan's Bar in Encino. Eddie already had his own table, after all, which was surrounded by a group of hangers-on. The office was always open, for some strange reason, commensurate with happy hour. We worked long, hard hours, so we could often be found at the office on Saturdays and Sundays too.

We were close on seed money a few times. But truthfully, we were usually being hustled by even greater bullshit artists than we were. But Eddie kept attracting people. He was, truly, one of the greatest storytellers I have ever met. Everyone within earshot was spellbound by his tales.

Maybe that's why even the mob considered funding us. No, not a mob. The mob.

They were rightfully indignant. One hundred twelve pounds of heroin is stolen from the police evidence locker and sold back to the public at a massive profit? They would've been happy—and quiet—if the heroin had gone to them. But it hadn't. And they wanted to clear their good name. An emissary was sent to Sonny Franzese's office, graciously offered rent-free at the Leavenworth federal prison. For some reason, he declined. Maybe because Eddie had put away so many of his business associates.

Somehow, we opened a real office across from CBS Studios in the Valley. We had plans and we had great support from actors and crew, all of whom were under Eddie's spell. They were willing to work for nothing, they said, and wanted only a proverbial "piece of the back end."

There never was a back end. Not for lack of trying. As his partner, I tried everything and took every meeting. A wife of a well-known swindler who raised dachshunds and helped her husband launder money through a kennel near Tijuana? Sure, I took that meeting. A well-known boxer who could hardly speak but would front cash for a guaranteed role? I took that meeting.

Then, finally, a real break: A lawyer in New York phoned and said he had investors. They wanted a meeting. I rushed to Houlihan's, our branch location. Eddie was surrounded by the usual wannabes.

"I got someone! A whole bunch of someones!" I declared.

Eddie was overjoyed. Especially since I was so sure. And even more so because I offered to pay my own way.

"Where you staying? I like the Wyndham. Across from the Plaza, very reasonable. And the Oyster House is just a block away."

Reasonable and oysters made sense. I boarded a plane the next day.

I walked into the lobby.

"Jesus, you kept me waiting," Eddie said, standing up. I had no idea how he got there that fast, but there he was. Off to our meeting, together. It couldn't fail.

Or maybe it could. And it did. It was poorly attended, to say the least. Even the lawyer who arranged it hadn't shown up. But walking down the street with Eddie in New York was an experience I'll never forget. Beat cops and cruisers stopped to shake his hand, like he was a celebrity. After the oysters, I went back to the hotel and Eddie went out on the town. He arrived back at the hotel penniless—the New York cop, the famous cop, had been mugged.

Did we make the movie? No. Was it worth it? Yes. Eddie moved to Florida and opened a bar, which he'd always wanted to do. He was more than just a cop who did (more or less accidentally) a lot of good: He was good. And sadly, like all the good ones, he died far too young. And Eddie was a real good guy.

Some Bad Guys
Are Also Good Guys

Domenic was a bad guy. I mean, a really bad guy. He had been a hit man for the mob. I met him for the first time in Los Angeles, when I hired him to build a barbecue in my backyard. One of his many talents—masonry. His other talents were intimidation, assault, and murder. He was an enforcer for Tony Provenzano, a capo in New York's Genovese family. He didn't confess that to me at first. Frankly, it would have been a terrible way to start a construction project. But once we got to know each other, he opened up. I was fascinated by Domenic. I had made a career playing characters like him. I tried to capture his strange high-pitched chuckle, his mannerisms, his idiosyncrasies. He was an incredible character: funny, violent, and yet very compassionate.

"You ever kill a guy?" I asked him once, as we lit our cigars.

"Yeah."

"Really? More than one?"

"Yeah."

I looked at him questioningly, in shocked silence.

"Twenty-two," he said, very matter-of-factly.

He had large hands, just massive paws, which I imagined he used to manhandle and hurt his victims. He had been a boxer, a middleweight contender, and later was a security guard at a bank. Even on that bank job, he tried to start a fight every day. He just liked to fight.

Domenic had a sense of justice too. He'd been ordered to kill the mistress of a man who thought his secret was soon to be made public. A standard assignment: eliminate the girlfriend. So he went to the mistress's house, pretending to be a friend of a friend. He waited on the stoop in the late afternoon. A woman got off the bus with a little girl in a Catholic school uniform. They started talking—she was a friendly woman.

"Hey, it's cold. Can we's go upstairs?" he asked after a bit.

The woman couldn't have been sweeter, and she welcomed him inside. She was cooking, and he was hypnotized by the aroma of sautéed clams. She sent her daughter to do some homework and asked Domenic if he'd like wine. How gracious.

"Would youse like to join us for dinner?" she asked.

"What do you got?"

"Vongole."

"Perfect."

The whole apartment was barely more than a room, and the window got all steamed up. As the room grew warm with the stove on, she took her sweater off. The mistress had a housedress on underneath. That's when Domenic saw the bruises.

"What's that?" he asked her.

"Nothing, it's nothing," she said, but she was clearly upset.
He insisted she tell him.

She'd gotten mixed up with the wrong guy, she explained.

"It's not all the time. Just sometimes, when he drinks . . ." She trailed off, trying to downplay it.

Domenic was enraged. Apparently, he had no problem with killing an innocent woman on behalf of a stranger. But he did take umbrage at the fact that his client had beaten this sweet woman now making this lovely meal. There was a code, Domenic's code, which had been broken.

"I forgot I have to run an errand," Domenic announced abruptly. "Keep it hot."

"Okay . . . ," she said, confused.

"I won't be long."

He went out, found the guy—his own client—and took care of him. Then he returned for his share of the linguine vongole. It was still warm.

Domenic's universe of morals was so twisted up, I never even knew where I stood with him. So one day, I asked him.

"Domenic, I'm just curious—if you got a contract to kill me, would you do it?"

He started to think about the question.

"No, Domenic, seriously. Do you really have to think about it that long? I'm supposed to be your friend."

Finally, he answered.

"Johnny, business is business," he said.

I stared at him in shocked silence.

"But I promise ya yous'ed never know I was there. I'd be right behind ya. You'd never know no fear."

Thanks, Dom. I feel *much* better now.

He had a young daughter with a disability to whom he was completely devoted, taking her to every doctor he could find, completely doting on her. And he had a profession that required him to have no remorse. After he died, his mistress contacted me. He had left me something, she said. It was a book of poetry with a page marked. The poem on that marked page was about the importance and value of friendship.

Be Happy with
What You Have

I instructed Captain Ed to prepare *Celebration,* my sixty-foot
Gulfstar sailboat, for a journey from Trinidad to Miami,
Florida, where she would be berthed for the remainder of
the season. Captain Ed and I had sailed through the Caribbean
often, though we'd never made a passage as long as this one. I
could have sailed on to Alaska. I didn't care. In that boat, which
I occasionally lived on throughout the years, I was so damn
happy. The boat seemed to deliver me mystical experiences.
Once, I was with Robert Styx, a director and professor of film
studies. We were sailing on the backside of Catalina during the
time when the whales were running. It was October, kind of
chilly. Full moon. We were drinking and having a good time.
The waves were huge: long rollers way out to sea, the land far
out of sight. We were heading out to San Nicolas, one of those
outer islands off the coast of California. All of a sudden there was
a roar and the boat rose fifteen feet in the air. A huge whale

exploded from the sea. He had surfaced to spy on us. His eye looked like a plate, brown and beautiful. In that eye, I could see the moon, swinging like a pearl. He went up, then splashed down with that magnificent tail. He hit the water like a freight train and we got drenched. We sat in stunned silence. If the creature had hit us with his tail, it would have smashed my boat and us with it. But at that moment, when I looked right into the whale's eye, there was a connection, and it was magical.

That boat was an endless adventure. I found her for sale in Myrtle Beach, South Carolina. She had a special history, once the personal yacht of the very talented designer and boat builder Bill Lazzara. She carried a full complement of sail. I don't remember the exact tonnage, but she was close to sixty thousand pounds, heavily built, designed to handle long and distant passages in comfort, safety, and luxury. In spite of her weight and sixteen-foot beam, she went to weather high and proud. She had some years on her, and it was a rare day when the air-conditioning, water maker, and refrigeration were all working at the same time. If the weather fax worked consistently, it might have spared us some close calls as we cruised between the islands on our way to and from Miami. She was strong, though, and her ability to handle a tempestuous, angry sea saved my life on two occasions.

This was one of those occasions.

I was an experienced sailor, but to properly handle a boat like *Celebration* and a long passage through the Caribbean, it would have been foolish to attempt the trip myself. A reliable captain is hard to find, and I was blessed to have Captain Ed. (He refused to go by anything else—I once called him Eddie and we almost came to blows.) Captain Ed was more than just the best sailor I've ever known. He had earned his doctorate in metallurgy and could repair most anything on the boat and off it. He was also a teacher. Listening to him tell his stories about traveling the world as a vagabond—like the time he worked the Alaska pipeline, hitch-hiked through India, found his way to an opium den in China, or survived an infestation of crabs in his eyebrows on a two-day bus trip through the Andes—were reminders to me that life should be lived fearlessly and passionately. Not so passionately that one ends up with crabs in one's eyebrows, perhaps, a story of which I never got the full details. Among my fondest memories of my time with Captain Ed were sharing the view of many starry skies at night under a Caribbean moon, and laughing about the time we were boarded at gunpoint by the Bahamian navy.

Here's what happened: We had forgotten to light the anchor lamp before going to sleep, and because our vessel had no mark-ings, the Bahamian navy suspected our dark ship of being a smuggling boat. Why else would we not have our lights on in these busy, very shallow waters? These Bahamian navy officers approached our boat with their guns raised. I sensed the com-manding officer had a sense of humor.

So I suggested it would be most unfair to shoot us both.

"Just shoot the captain," I said, pointing at Ed.

We defused the situation with a few gifted bottles of rum and a case of beer, which we proceeded to drink together. The navy officer was even kind enough to let me photograph Captain Ed in their handcuffs, between two huge crewmen with their ma-chine guns. We finished our beers, saluted our new friends, and sailed on. These were among the best days of my life, out to sea with a stiff breeze right on the beam, making eight to nine knots, the rigging humming a symphony of joy. Beside us, porpoises galloped across the sea like puppies at play and birds glided in muted adagio against a painted sky.

As I had discovered so many years ago driving across the country, moonlight was my favorite watch. Alone on deck, tethered to the binnacle if the waters were rough, the shooting stars were so close I found myself ducking at times. It was wondrous to contemplate the vastness, infinity, and my own mortality. These nights were exquisite, and looking at these glowing, brilliant stars, many that had given up their lives centuries ago, always made me think of just how small and fragile I was. Sometimes those night watches caused me much melancholy. I wondered, amid all that beauty, how could one be sad? No matter how encompassing the darkness, it always gave way to the brightness of the morning.

We made a leg east to Miami via the Virgin Islands. We should never have left the comforts of a marina in Saint Lucia. There was a massive storm ahead. But we had no way of knowing—as usual, our weather fax was not working. But had we not sailed into near doom, I would have been deprived of a chance meeting with a truly most interesting man.

We were on a good reach somewhere east of Saint Lucia between Antigua and Martinique. The day was clear with a light breeze. We seldom turned on the engine, even if the winds were fair—the grinding sounds of that iron jenny were such an intrusion on the senses. Interrupting the murmuring wind in the rigging was a sacrilege.

We trolled a line for fish when the going was slow enough,

and at midmorning Captain Ed caught an impressive wahoo, which we were looking forward to grilling that evening. Much like the weather fax, the refrigerator was not working, but there was ice in the chest. In went the fish until evening.

In fact, it would be two days before I saw that beautiful fish again.

By midafternoon, the air had taken on a more menacing demeanor. Captain Ed checked the barometer. It was starting to drop. Not a good sign. Earlier, we had seen a few thunderstorms on the horizon, but they were small and scattered. The winds were easterly and the clouds to the west were not so much a concern. As the afternoon progressed, we figured, the weather would continue to move farther away.

We figured wrong. Soon the storm clouds started building, stacking themselves on top of one another like a huge layer cake, obscuring the sun. The squall line advanced, the barometer dropped precipitously, and then an ominous silence fell upon us. We knew what was coming: a dangerous squall. We immediately dropped sail and hoisted the storm jib. We went around the deck, lashing everything down, put on our foul-weather gear, and laid out the safety lines—fore and aft—and attached tethers. It was now time to secure below. But we'd run out of time. We could smell it—that unmistakable electrical odor of lightning about to strike. And then it did, stabbing the building sea with a vengeance.

It was time to turn on the engine. We'd need to have better steerage in the roiling, directionless sea. The wind then picked up and started to batter us, gusting up to forty knots and then faster. Captain Ed tried turning over the engine. No luck. And then tried again to no avail. Make that three things that weren't working on the boat that day. Wonderful. We were now running under bare poles and heading downwind with a high sea on our ass.

Then our electrical went out. We were now a ghost ship screaming downwind, barely under control, and with no instrumentation. We couldn't get below, the cockpit had taken on water, and we were weary, hungry, and hoping the storm gods would offer us a small respite.

Two exhausting days later, toward the late afternoon, the wind dropped as if it had fallen asleep. The sea turned calm, and the dark skies above us broke and revealed a pastel tapestry above that drenched us in sunlight and warmth. We were ecstatic and spent. We'd been at the mercy of the wind for days. Our food supplies were running dangerously low. Sleep had been impossible under those conditions, though on the second night I thought I dozed off. Or perhaps I was delusional. Or dreaming. Storms play funny tricks on the mind.

But we'd been pardoned. With the storm gone, we stretched out on the warm decks, the sun bringing my sore arms and legs back to life better than any masseuse. Occasionally, we'd peel ourselves up from the deck to look around. We were now lost somewhere in the Caribbean. There was no land in sight, no other ship visible. To celebrate such beauty and our survival, we fished out a bottle of rum that we'd kept from our layover in Saint Lucia, chased it down with a can of guava juice, and fell back on the decks, dead asleep.

At twilight, we woke and undertook a brief inventory of the ship. We'd lost a man-overboard ring and pole, the water-activated strobe attached to it, two jerry cans, and, perhaps most important, a sea chart that covered our area and alerted us to any foreign objects like shipwrecks and fluctuations in depth, which this part of the sea was known for. Where we were, it was not unusual to sail the reefs with only a few feet of water below at one moment and a few hundred fathoms the next. That missing sea chart would have done us no good anyway, because we had no idea where we were. Our instruments were still out of whack, and it was still so rough we couldn't keep a running fix.

But we were alive.

On the horizon, we were able to make out what appeared to be a cay, or small island. The Caribbean was dotted with cays—hurricane holes, they were called—places where sailors could seek refuge from fierce storms. Some had docks and room for a few boats.

We had to dock. We needed to rest up and make a few repairs. The winds were picking up again, so we put up a light sail and ghosted over to the small island. It was not wise to drop anchor without a proper chart, but ours had been snatched up by the storm. Our best hope was to find a resting place in the lee of the island. If we were lucky, perhaps we could find an access point to the interior. If there was one.

It was dark now. By flashlight, we scanned the coastline of the cay and cautiously entered an opening on the jungle shore—no easy feat in unknown waters without an engine. From time to time we were bumping the bottom. Soon the shoreline opened up and we spotted a run-down quay with a place for us to dock. Getting close would be hard. We figured we'd have only one pass at it, because if we missed the dock, there was no room to tack about or maneuver to safety.

I dove into the water and, with a quickly thrown spring line, managed to stop our momentum. Onboard, Captain Ed put the bumpers down. At long last, this phase of our journey was over. But where were we? We rocked turbulently in the ghostlike port. The moon was rising, and we thought we saw a dim light winking through the dense jungle foliage not too far away.

"Anybody there?" I called out.

Nothing. Then:

"Hello, my friend."

I looked to Ed, wondering who was coming for us. My mind was spinning from fatigue and hunger, my face tight and dry from saltwater. I remembered a book from my childhood about a handful of stowaways who were picked up by islanders who turned out to be cannibals. Would Captain Ed and I suffer the same fate? A pirogue was now heading our way. Inside, a tall, lean man was paddling, his teeth gleaming in the moonlight.

"I am Jarmin," he said proudly, carefully tying up alongside us. Inside his skiff I could see our friend was barefoot, and his ragged T-shirt flapped in the wind like clothing on a line. He was uncharacteristically tall, his height accentuated by his slim stature and long black hair tied back in an island version of a chignon. His height, he later explained, was due to his Masai ancestry, his father having been a great warrior. He was not alone. Standing tall in the bow of his boat was his sole companion: the General, a red-tailed rooster that was as scrawny and disheveled as Jarmin was.

We thanked Jarmin for his kind welcome and explained the events leading up to our arrival. We were very hungry and asked if he knew of a local restaurant or perhaps a store where we could purchase provisions. We had our doubts—the island itself was pitch-black and looked uninhabited. Jarmin appeared deep in thought as he considered our request, then announced that he knew of a very fine place for us, and not too far away. There was no sense in changing into dry clothes, as we were in an open boat and it had started to rain anyway, so we gingerly boarded his narrow, beamed canoe with the ancient little outboard motor and the General crowing into the night wind. We slipped out through the mouth of the island as Jarmin steered us to our next destination.

Soon enough, we were again on the open sea, tossed about in large rollers, remnants of the storm. We were now at the mercy of our new friend, who fortunately was a fine seaman and kept his humble skiff upright. After an hour or so at sea, Jarmin announced that we were close. It had started to rain when another island appeared. Jarmin steered on through the mouth of a small river and started to whistle as we glided through the jungle. The rain stopped, the wind abated, and the stars blinked open again.

The inlet grew larger as we glided along in silence, in a quiet so welcome after days of howling winds and on water that was finally flat. In the moonlight, against the remains of an old fuel dock that was leaning against the shoreline, we could see a few boats. Civilization! The smell of kerosene lamps and blooming night jasmine all blended together on this warm tropical evening, and we heard the sounds of dogs barking and voices in the distance. With Jarmin at the helm and the General keeping watch, our skiff moved toward the sounds in the darkness. We passed a beach with small fishing boats resting against the sand and shacks that had seen better days.

A creaky dock appeared, and behind it we could hear the beat of music. Jarmin beached the boat near the others, and we followed him and the General (conveniently perched on Jarmin's shoulder) for a few hundred yards. The moon was now out, full in the starry sky, casting a light bright enough to read a newspaper by. The beach gave way to a slow-moving stream. We waded through the water, which carried us between large outcroppings of rock, mountains coming out of the shoreline. We kept following the river, which flowed from the entrance of a large cave, and arrived at our destination. It was a magical place.

The grotto had a waterfall tumbling down the large rock face, and the cave revealed itself like a cathedral. The rooms and outposts all glittered with candlelight. Tables and benches surrounded a luminescent pool of crystal-clear water. In it were the reflections of flickering candles and moonbeams, which found their way through little fissures in the cavernous rock and sparkled. The ceiling stood fifty feet high, perhaps higher.

The cave had been converted into a first-class restaurant of sorts. Our fellow diners sat at different levels on the rock, some in first-class yacht finery, some in shorts and bare feet. The acoustics were wonderfully kind to the ears. I looked for the kitchen, which was built half inside the grotto and produced the most wonderful aroma of roasting treasures from the sea, fresh bread, and pork. The grill was open to the air, and three cooks were lined up at the hip and turning out masterpieces on what looked like an old laundry stove. Above them, hanging on spikes that had been anchored into the stone, was an odd assortment of pots, pans, and utensils. Like the patrons, nothing matched.

A handsome fellow with the look of a pirate appeared and waved us to a table of stone. Down below, sitting in the water, a few folks sipped cocktails.

I turned around to thank Jarmin for showing us this truly wondrous place, but he and the General had held back.

"Come and join us," I said, waving him on.

He politely refused.

"Wait a second, my friend. We will not eat without our captain," I said.

Jarmin let that sink in a moment and, liking his new billing, agreed to join us.

We put in our orders, and Jarmin told us a little about the history of the island. It didn't have an official name, though it went by many, depending on who you were asking. It prospered with very little: a small marina, a fuel dock, a few mechanics whose skills were legendary, and, outside of a few restaurants and the local fishermen who supplied them, nothing else. In total, the population was in the hundreds.

It was a safe place to ride out bad weather, and some knowledgeable mariners left their boats there throughout the hurricane season. Years later, that sadly all changed, when a devastating storm hit hard. The only place left was the grotto.

Our dinner came out slowly, like everything else in the tropics, but the diversity of flavors and a combination of French, Portuguese, Spanish, and Creole were well represented. Like everything else in that place, none of the dishes matched: Eggplant and salt fish, baked bread (buttery and light), mangoes, guava, and the tiny very sweet Antiguan pineapples. Then came goat stew wrapped in palm leaves and drenched in warm coconut milk. We were given samples of local cheese, thanks to the goats, and the pièces de résistance: conch fritters, grilled red snapper, and huge lobsters. The island beer and rum were served in tin cans of various sizes. Much was salvaged from debris left from past storms and shipwrecks. The whole island was like that, jerry-rigged together with shards of others' misfortunes, dreams picked over in their resting place and left behind for salvagers here to uncover. Gifts from the storm gods.

We made a toast with our tin cans and laughed at our predicament. We'd reached this most magnificent place and had no idea where we even were. Tucked away in a hurricane hole somewhere east of Saint Lucia was our best guess. We had been without navigational instruments for days, and we were so hungry—and so taken with our new friend Jarmin—we hadn't bothered to plot our new position once we'd landed. We'd been taken to this magical place we didn't know, and could likely never find again without the help of our new friend and his pet rooster. It was wonderful, too wonderful to be true. But it was true. I proposed another toast.

It was well after midnight when we finished. We found our scrawny canoe and returned to our ship. We were feeling no pain. That night I slept as never before on the deck, in a fragrant tropical breeze. It was one of the best evenings of my life. I didn't even hear Ed's snoring, which was reminiscent of the entire San Diego Zoo during mating season.

The next morning I felt humbled. There was so much about sailing I loved in those days: the beauty of the skies, the texture of the wind, the solitude so far from shore. Wherever we were.

I liked to greet each day with a simple affirmation, written by a dear friend.

> *I wish to honor the miracle of life within me and*
> *   around me*
> *To promote the bounty and beauty of creation.*
> *Help me to be a faithful servant and witness to the*
> *   light of love, freedom, joy, equanimity.*
> *To always search for truth and forgiveness*
> *For myself and all others.*

I had had the pleasure of learning much from that friend in my pursuit of truth and wisdom on my personal journey. Or at least I tried to learn. The sun was just rising; all was still. Just sitting on the warm deck surrounded by the jungle and tranquil sea, I quietly repeated the affirmation. And then I dove into the water. What a glorious way to greet the morning.

Meanwhile, Captain Ed had opened the hatches and the sunlight poured in. After the storm, it was great to dry out at last. Down below, he'd found our problem in the engine room. At least one of them. It was the usual diagnosis: contaminated diesel fuel. The filters were cleaned and replaced. The air-conditioning unit, bilge pump, and water maker were not such an easy fix, however, and we'd need more time to repair them.

As we worked to repair the boat, Jarmin, our savior, appeared in his skiff and greeted us again with his laughter, along with the General, whose mangy feathers were rather dazzling in the morning light. We enjoyed a breakfast onboard of local bread, butter, and freshly picked papaya. Even though we were strangers, we spoke with Jarmin as if we were old mates.

After coffee, Ed returned to the various repairs we needed to make and Jarmin volunteered to show me his home. We walked along the jungle path. In the distance, he pointed. It was humble, to be sure. It was a shack, a collage of flotsam that had been blown up onto the beach. Driftwood of varying sizes. Boards of all shapes. If these puzzle pieces didn't fit together and create protection against the elements, he simply placed another over the structure's irregular seams. Tarps of various colors were placed among this odd assortment of debris, and in unique formations.

"Why are there gaps?" I asked.

"To let the big winds pass through," he said.

I remembered a trip to Hong Kong, where I'd seen how architects had designed modern skyscrapers with upper floors that were entirely open, allowing the heavy winds of typhoons and monsoons to pass through. And here, on this little island, thousands of miles away, Jarmin had done the same.

He ushered me inside his shack. The interior was a good-size room that had been divided into quarters by tarps. On the wall, there was a crucifix hanging between faded pictures of John Wayne (who had shot me in the head several times) and John F. Kennedy. Along one wall was a bookshelf of sorts, and the bed was an eclectic assortment of cushions that looked as though they'd been plucked from old yachts. Hanging above us was a once beautiful ship wheel, and swinging in the breeze throughout the yard was a collection of ship bells that chimed over the sound of gentle waves with an ethereal loveliness. Jarmin showed me the kitchen, another graveyard of reclaimed items.

There was an old refrigerator, though how it ever ran was unclear considering there was no electricity or generator in sight. It was not needed, as he revealed the smoker he had built inside. Whatever washed ashore that had some value seemed to make it into Jarmin's home.

He had no running water, which was fine because he had arranged his incredible tarps to capture the afternoon downpour so common in the tropics, allowing him to fill his fifty-gallon drums. He never ran out. The floor was dirt, with the ubiquitous tarps arranged over whatever area was muddiest. He had chickens as well—the General's harem—but they were allocated to an outside coop, which stood next to his marijuana plants. The chickens seemed very happy.

"Best on the island," he said, with understandable pride.

I asked him about hot water. Where did he bathe?

"Hot water is not good for the skin," he said, explaining that he bathed in the sea or in the rain, which kept his hair shiny and soft.

I then noticed his toilet seat. It was hanging from a banyan tree like a child's swing. He could move it whenever he wanted and for whatever reason: according to the prevailing winds or rain, or if he just wanted to change the view.

"This is where I pray," he said, showing me the porch.

"When do you pray?"

"I have to be in the mood," he said.

"What do you pray to?" I asked.

"To this beautiful place," he said, raising his hands to his home, "and then the entire island, and the sea, the wind, too, the fruit trees, the chickens, the sun, the stars, the moon."

How lucky, I thought, that Jarmin had become my friend. After visiting his incredible home, I concluded there really wasn't much missing in his life except taxes, traffic, and other people's noise. Perhaps he was the most successful man I had ever met. No money, few possessions to worry about losing, no ambition but to be kind to strangers who might seek his help as we did that stormy night. Two days later, as we were about to cast off, he handed me a small package. Inside was a slip of paper with a mailing address (he hoped it would work but wasn't sure) and a surprise gift: a bracelet made from rooster feathers, a memento I treasure. Even now, so many years later, it remains a reminder of its wise creator and the lesson he taught me: true luxury is a life well lived.

The Only Thing You
Can't Make More of Is Time

My life was a nonstop hustle, busy with my growing business (one that I would later lose, a story for another book), when I learned my father was traveling west for a fishing trip. Herbert Avrutus, his friend and the doctor who delivered me, had a cabin in Butte, Montana. I decided to clear out for a few days and join them, as it was considered among the finest places to fly-fish.

But it was not my father's favorite. He'd always loved the Margaree River, up in Nova Scotia, where he caught a monster salmon on the first day he was there—and never again in his life. He came back with a tam-tam hat that he wore on the rivers from then on, and which I still wear today. One day, we promised, we'd return together to fish the Margaree.

I drove from Los Angeles to Butte, wondering if this might be the last time I'd ever see him. He was getting older, the aches turning to illnesses, and had some light dementia. It was hard for me to see him that way, to grow old with him, a reminder of the ticking time bomb of life. He had been so vivacious for so long.

As I drove, I remembered a time my father came to visit me in Los Angeles. He came often during the winters, spending a month at a time. While he never met Fernando Lamas, we spent a lot of time with Esther Williams, his widow. I remained friendly with her. When she was invited to parties and events, I'd accompany her. She was such a lovely woman, and she met my family when they'd come out for their winter visit. Once, we met up with Esther and went to dinner at Le Restaurant, a famous place back then. We picked her up and I drove their car, Fern's old Rolls-Royce, through Beverly Hills. We were all having a blast. We had the volume up on the radio, listening to swing music, and passed the famous fountain near the Beverly Hills Hotel.

"How about a dance?" my father asked her.

"But of course," she said.

I pulled the car over, we opened the doors of the Rolls and put the music on even higher; my father and Esther got out, and he started dancing with her around the fountain.

My father was a wonderful dancer. He could buck and do a swing and a wicked Charleston. I watched them there I felt so proud of how far I'd come. In the eyes of my father, now dancing with Esther Williams in his arms, moving with her around a fountain in Beverly Hills, his feet gliding and a smile across his face, this was success. We were living life at the fullest, together.

But now our time was short. I arrived in Butte and we fished for days. The Jackson and the Jefferson as well as some smaller streams. We had the best time, laughing together as we always had. Perhaps we laughed a little harder. After all, how many more chances would there be?

On the last day of the trip, as the day was growing late, I was getting anxious. Storm clouds swirled above us in the big sky. Even though I had grown and had children of my own, I didn't want to leave him. I was thinking, "Jesus, I have to say good-bye to him." I really didn't want to. I never did.

When I was a child, after my escape from Phelps, my father was the one who was forced to take me back. I had been used to my mother leaving me. But that day, driving up the driveway at that school, I couldn't hold back the tears. And neither could he. When he drove away that day, that hit me harder than I had ever been hit—before or since. It took me a long time to come to terms with that moment of abandonment by my father, despite the fact that he had little choice. Now here I was, a man, having to do the same to him. Just toward sunset, when the evening hatch was on, the time came to part ways.

"You better get going," he said as we walked up the dark riverbed.

"I know," I said. I thought about staying another day to be close to him, so we could just keep fishing, so I didn't have to say good-bye. But I knew that postponing the trip wasn't the right thing to do either. All things must come to an end.

He turned and we hugged. I kissed him on the cheek, smelling his old Bay Rum aftershave and Palmolive soap. I put my arm around him. We stood silently for a moment, together, in that magnificent place. And then we split. He walked up the stream. I couldn't move. I just watched as he ambled away. He paused once and turned around to check on me. He waved a final good-bye and then disappeared.

I was fortunate to see him again, but he wasn't the same. He was sleeping more and more. He'd stopped his daily one-mile hike. He was living in upstate New York in his pre-revolutionary farmhouse. A few years earlier, I had built a house nearby so we could stay close. I was coming back from the airport in Albany and I stopped by to see him as I always did. He was eating his favorite lunch: lox and a bagel. He wasn't hungry. I ate half.

He usually delighted in hearing my stories from the road, proud that he had a son who was making "serious money," who was a success. But this day, he said he was tired and wanted to take a nap. He got into bed and closed his eyes, so content.

I sat there, watching him for some time, thinking about our life together. All that he had taught me. All that he had done for me. I got into his bed and put my arms around him. After a few minutes, he opened his eyes.

"Hey, kid," he said.

"Yeah?" I said.

"Next spring, we ought to fish the Margaree," he said.

"We will, Pop. I promise."

A smile came over his face.

"I love you, Pop."

"I know you do. I love you too, son."

And then he drifted off.

We never did fish the Margaree.

.　.　.

I scattered some of his ashes in the Green River in Vermont, where we spent so many wonderful days fishing together. I visit there from time to time, and when I do the memories come flooding back like the water that runs through the riverbed. The rest of his ashes I keep in his tackle box—the one with the little vise for tying those elegant fishing flies to match the hatch.

He lived to fish. It's a pretty great thing to live for. I also believe he lived to love. I know he loved me, and he knew I loved him.

I think that's a pretty great thing to live for too.

FINALE

G oldsmith?" the casting agent said.

The wait was over. I walked into the studio. It was cold, dark, and empty. At the center of the stage was an illuminated chair, and I took my seat there, surveying the space. I had never been in a casting room like this. It was a strange environment for casting. No props. No actors or casting personnel to read with. No one to throw you a line or even a smile. I could see only a camera mounted high on the wall, amid a bank of recording equipment. The box was sending a live video feed back to New York, where the director, the agency executives, and the client were all watching.

"One moment," someone said from a speaker, a voice that was so distant it could have been beamed down to me from the moon.

I was annoyed at the entire operation, and sitting there and waiting for the audition to begin, I decided to remove my shoe and sock. Maybe that would get their goddamned attention.

The speaker came on again, filling the studio with reverb that echoed in the empty room. It was the director this time.

"I see that you took your sock off," he said. "Why?"

Somewhere, in that moment, it all hit me. I had everything I needed to do this. I had been preparing for this role my whole life. I had almost died at sea and on a mountain. I had met Jarmin and Grace and Eddie Egan and Domenic and Joan Fontaine. I had been caught naked on a freeway in LA and had debunked a miracle worker in the Philippines. Granted, I had never arm-wrestled Fidel

Castro. But it wasn't out of the realm of possibility that, with one slightly different turn, I could have.

Just make 'em laugh, I thought. And then I began channeling my late friend Fernando Lamas, mimicking his Argentinean accent and sentence structure. Everyone always laughed at my Fernando jokes.

"Don't you peoples know?" I said indignantly. "This is what's called an icebreaker. See, amigo? You asked me, didn't you?"

Inside the booth, I could hear the echo of laughter.

"Tell us about your life," he said.

I scratched my beard and looked up.

"Well, it's a wonderful life," I said.

"How did you start out?"

"When I was a little boy, I wanted to be a hunter," I said. "I used to hang around in Abercrombie's gun room and look at these beautiful animals. Don't get me wrong, I love animals. But you know, I was only going to kill the bad ones. I knew all about it. I even made and hand-loaded my own bullets. And that's what I wanted to do, until I discovered Lucy."

"Who's Lucy?" the director asked.

"You don't know about Lucy?" I said increduously.

"No."

"Well, Lucy was a beautiful girl in the sixth grade. And I had a fancy for her, you know."

"So, what happened?" the director asked.

"You know what happened," I said matter of factly. "I was an early starter."

Behind the camera box, I could hear the agency people failing to stifle their laughter. Down on the floor, I knew it. I had them. I was in control. They never shut the box again.

"What happened with your career?" the director asked.

"Well, after Lucy, I discovered the womens. I changed my mind about my career."

"What did you want to do?"

"I wanted to be an ob-gyn."

"How old were you?"

"Maybe around eleven," I said, relishing now the laughs I could hear from the booth.

"How did you get to meet Fidel?" the director asked.

"Well, I thought that you knew about that. You people seem to know about everything. I tell you. I was a runaway. A truant. One day, I fell asleep on a fucking train and I found myself in the Sierra Madre."

"What were you doing there?" the director asked.

"I was hunting for the wild and elusive Litvak," I said without batting an eyelash. "One day, I came upon a river and I see these ladies and they're doing their laundry in the river."

"Well, what did you do?"

"What do you think I did? I fucked them all."

"Just straight like that?"

"Absolutely," I said, straight-faced. "I fucked them all, and I got quite a reputation because, well, I was incredible."

"So how did you meet Fidel?"

"Well, if you peoples let me finish, I tell you. It was through Che. Che Guevara. You know him, right?"

"Really. How did you come to know Che?"

"I rode with him. I let him borrow my motorcycle."

"You did?"

"Yeah, because he wanted me to fuck one of his younger

sisters, to be introduced to being a lady by someone who knew what he was doing. I was honored."

"You were that good?"

"You know, you must read the newspapers in those days. The word, it traveled fast. I met the womens. There was lots of womens and they passed me around. They think that they own me. I let them own me. I have an obligation, because I developed, you know, some special techniques."

"What kind of techniques?"

"Well, I don't think that I want to tell you peoples," I said, and as the laughter continued and they took another conference, I became panic-stricken about my truck. Forget about the ticket and fine. My monologue had been going on for so long, I worried the truck could have been towed. La Brea is a busy street. But they wanted to continue.

"And Fidel?"

"And Fidel heard about me," I said, "because I fucked his mistress's sister, and of course I had to fuck her too."

"You fucked them all?"

"Of course, I fucked everybody."

"And what happened?"

"So he challenged me to a duel," I said. "Fidel didn't like the fact that I fucked his mistress or her sister, so he wants to get the pistols. I told him, 'Fidel, we can get the pistols if you want, but no sense in hurting ourselves. How about we play chess? It's painless.' He agreed. So we play chess and I let him win. He gets very upset. He wants to beat me fair and says, 'Well, we have one more contest, amigo. The arm-wrestle.' And that's how I arm-wrestled Fidel Castro."

They were in hysterics.

. . .

I ran for my truck, expecting to see an empty parking space. It was still there—I hadn't been towed yet. I got in the truck to head back to the campground. But first I called Barbara, my new agent. I was upset. It had seemed like the audition went well, but I was still convinced I wasn't the right type for the part.

"Honey, you made a mistake," I said. "I'm all wrong for this. Don't waste their time, my time, and your time. It ain't going to work."

"You're a good actor," she said. "Keep the faith and let's forget about it. It's out of our hands now."

Time went by and I nearly did forget about it. But then I was called back. And there were just two of us. I knew the final audition had been one of my best performances.

"He was terrific!" Joe Blake, the casting director, told us the following day.

Barbara agreed with Blake. We were ecstatic.

"There's just one problem," Blake told us. "They think they might want to go younger."

Foiled again, I thought, and so heartbreakingly close! How could I put myself in a position to be so crushed? Just like all the close calls before.

Barbara was furious.

"Joe, this doesn't make any sense at all," she said. "How can you possibly be interesting if you're young?"

Her rationale made sense. To be interesting, you have to have had experiences. And to have had experiences, you needed time. And I had spent a lot of time having a hell of a time.

"Let me call you back," Blake said, and he called the agency and client to make our case. The next day, I started my career as the Most Interesting Man in the World, a role I had been rehearsing for all my life.

Epilogue

T he Most Interesting Man in the World. I could have been
billed as the Luckiest Man in the World. In the years that
would follow, the most common question I was asked
was, "Why do you think the commercials were so successful?"
After all, they were. The character became a phenomenon, going
viral on the Internet the way few commercial campaigns have
before or since.

My answer? I think they made people smile.

I got the accolades. But I know that it never would have
happened without the incredible young talents who created the
brilliant campaign, one that won every award in its field. I will
always be grateful to them and the many talented people who
worked, wrote, and designed throughout my run.

And finally, after all those years trying to make it in Hollywood, I became a recognizable star. Even though I wasn't a lead
in major motion pictures, the popularity of my character offered

me some incredible experiences. Once, I was in a restaurant in Los Angeles, and I noticed a man approaching me, tall and imposing. He hesitantly and respectfully asked, "Could I get a picture with you?"

It was Michael Jordan, the basketball player and one of the biggest commercial celebrities ever. And he was asking me for a photo opportunity.

On another occasion, Leonardo DiCaprio crossed another restaurant to shake my hand. This was not early in his career— he was a bona fide star, and one who was not easily impressed. Yet there he was, coming to me like a wide-eyed kid. Less than a month later, I was in that same restaurant and had the same thing happen to me, only this time with Jennifer Lawrence.

"You're the Most Interesting Man in the World!"

If she said so. We had a very nice conversation about Hollywood and how it's changed. And how it hasn't. There is such a shared experience that comes from the rejections and the successes to be had there, and the wild artistry and the unique business environment, that we were able to connect even though we were decades apart in age.

I even got to thank Warren Beatty in person for all the help with the ladies he unknowingly gave me so many years before at the Beverly Wilshire Hotel. My son David was working crew on one of his movies. He told him my story and mentioned who I was and Beatty was a fan of the campaign and said he'd love to meet me. Soon after, we did meet, exchanging stories from our very different perspectives on Hollywood through the sixties, seventies, and eighties.

I've also been able to use my celebrity for good. I've worked with Mines Advisory Group, an organization that removes old but still active mines and bombs in the jungles of Vietnam, Cambodia, and other parts of the world. I work with Caring Canines, a service-dog organization. With Willy, my Anatolian shepherd, who's certified for service, by my side, we visit local old-age homes and the VA hospital. I am presently the proud chairperson of Make-A-Wish Vermont, which helps lift the spirits of children suffering from debilitating and life-threatening diseases in our state. Sometimes, when I see how the joy these young people experience can ease their pain and heal their physical maladies, I think back to Dr. Benji in the Philippines. Maybe we *can* heal with the mind. Maybe laughter, joy, elation, good friends, and a few wild adventures can make us better. If there is one thing I have learned in my long journey, it's that life is far too serious to take seriously. I hope it's something that you, my dear reader, learn as soon as possible.

I have had so many experiences since the start of the roller coaster that was the Dos Equis campaign. They are too numerous to detail here, but there is one of note: Perhaps the most incredible encounter was when I, in my seventies, returned to camp to play once more with bows and arrows, as I had so many years before with my father.

This time, the camp was Camp David. I was a birthday surprise for President Barack Obama.

The first time I met President Obama, I was part of a welcoming committee in the state of Vermont, where I reside. He was starting his second run for presidency, and we were invited to be in a greeting line of about two hundred people. Barbara, my agent, who was by then also my wife, was right when she said he would recognize me: He is a big sports fan, and the campaign ran heavily on ESPN. Our ten-second photo op turned into a several-minute conversation.

I thought, This must be a setup. Someone has to be playing a joke on me, and they prompted him with information. But when he mentioned that he loved a *New Yorker* feature about me that had been printed a year earlier and quoted from the commercials, I knew this was serious. I drove home feeling as if it were a dream. The president of the United States was interested in me.

Six months or so later, I got a call from one of his deputies at the White House. Would I like to be part of a special celebration for the president on his birthday? Ten of Obama's best friends in the world—friends from high school and grade school, mostly—were to be in attendance. And me, chosen as his surprise guest. All top secret.

You bet I would.

The Secret Service picked me up at Reagan National Airport, and a few hours later I was at Camp David, the president's private retreat, usually reserved for visiting heads of state. Frankly, I would have thought they would have chosen George Clooney, who is not only a huge movie star but also a good friend of Obama's and a fund-raiser for the Democratic Party. I just hoped the president wouldn't be disappointed.

There was to be fun and games all weekend, sporting events like bowling, riflery, and more. And archery. The president was set to arrive momentarily. Wanting to make a strong first impression, I thought of what my father had done in those woods at our camp so many years ago. I picked up five or six shafts and went over to the target and stuck them together in a tight cluster near the bull's-eye. Then I went back to the shooting position and stood with a bow and a single arrow as I inspected my "work."

I could hear the president coming with an aide.

"Damn," the president said in a half-hushed whisper, "this guy's good."

I turned around and, feigning bemused resentment, said, "What took you so long?"

He clapped his hands and laughed. He could not have been nearly as happy and amazed as I was to be there. I was to meet him two more times, once at the White House Correspondents' Dinner and once in the Oval Office.

The former was brief; the latter was as well, but it left me with something even more tangible than an incredible memory. I had been asked by the president's personal photographer, Pete Souza, to have lunch. Unfortunately, the day before our scheduled meeting, there was the tragic terrorist attack at the *Charlie Hebdo* office in Paris. I was sure the lunch would be canceled, as I assumed that the president and his photographer would be on their way to Paris.

The lunch was on, however. But I was informed that, for obvious reasons, the president would not attend or even make an appearance. After lunch, Pete asked if I would like to see the Oval Office. I jumped at the opportunity. What an awesome sense of wonder and history just to step inside such a place. Here was Roosevelt's chair for the fireside chats. Here was the bust of Martin Luther King Jr. The desk, a gift from the queen.

Suddenly, the doors swung open and energy filled the room. It was the president. He saw me.

"What are you doing here?" he asked.

"I came to give you this," I said, thinking fast, reaching into my jacket pocket and producing a Cuban cigar. "And what are you doing here?" I asked the president.

"Hey, man. I work here," he said. "I came to give you this."

It was a little blue jewelry box. Inside were gold presidential cuff links.

I pull them out from time to time. I wonder if they are real gold. But I would never have them appraised. I already know their value. To me, like so many memories, experiences, people, and places that I have had in my life, they are priceless.

Acknowledgments

This book is finished, but hopefully the story continues for a good while yet, filled with more adventures, misadventures, escapades, friendships, and, most of all, the interesting people without whom life would certainly not be the same.

If I'm being honest, I wish this all hadn't taken so long. But, then again, maybe if success had come earlier it wouldn't have meant as much as it does now. (And, of course, it would have given me more chances to screw it up.) The harder knocks, disappointments, and travails one has, the more opportunity one has to gain awareness of who the devil we really are. I'm still trying.

As I look back and reminisce over my journey and contemplate surviving the turbulence and difficulties inherent in all our lives to becoming a successful actor and, hopefully and more important, a successful man, I have many people to thank.

First, of course, is "the Coach," my dear father, Milton, without whom your author would never have been. His advice to a little boy many years ago to "never give up" has sustained and driven me all these years.

To all those who told me no, a special thanks. You also drove me on, giving me the resolve to determine my own worth, pursue my own dreams, and define my own destiny.

To my many friends and fans: Thanks for your kind thoughts and support, without which success would have been not only more elusive but devoid of any real meaning.

To my dogs, who have taught me much about unconditional love and simple joys, and to those few horses in Hollywood who didn't throw me: my heartfelt gratitude.

To the Reverend Steve Berry, who opened my heart and eyes to the mysteries of life.

To John McEntee, my booking agent, who is always looking out for me, far beyond the realm of booking.

To Chris Budden at Havas Agency, for his friendship.

To the advertising creatives Brandon Henderson, Karl Lieberman, and Jeff Kling, who came up with the Most Interesting Man in the World campaign: Though I have gotten the accolades and recognition, you are the unsung heroes. I trust by now you have moved out of your parents' basements and have gone on to other interesting campaigns worthy of your talents.

Through its tenure, there were copywriters, art directors, account leads, producers, clients, and so many more who dedicated themselves to the development of the advertising campaign. I am indebted to them all. They are too numerous to name, but two deserve special mention: the director, Steve Miller, and the entire crew at Radical Media, who helped to craft the look, feel, and tone of the campaign and made filming a joy for nearly ten years. And the mad genius Paul Fix, who, as creative director, helmed the campaign for nearly four years and then helped me in the construction, organization, and completion of my own story. Thanks always for your rare talent and friendship.

And, speaking of my own story, a sincere thank-you to Bryan Bender, the young and talented writer—then at *The Boston Globe*, now at *Politico*—who, after interviewing me upon my return from Vietnam, suggested I had a story to tell. He got the ball rolling for this book. Bryan, your ongoing friendship is so appreciated.

To Captain Ed Aigeltinger for the adventures and close calls.

To my wonderful lawyer, Ailleen Gorospe. My dear buddies for the good times: Tony, Les, Bob, Clark, Eric, and Jamie.

To Jill Schwartzman, my editor, and her crew at Dutton, especially Jamie Knapp, Andrea Monagle, and Marya Pasciuto, thanks for all your support, friendship, and hard work.

Special thanks to the inimitable Marcus Wiley, my business partner and dear friend, for his guidance, good taste, and innate ability to smooth the road on this lovely ride.

To my children, David, Drew, Cory, Jillian, and Karrie: You are my inspiration, who I think of more than you know.

And of course my wife, Barbara the Empress, who has had so much to do with my good fortune.

ABOUT THE AUTHOR

Jonathan Goldsmith grew up in the Bronx, trained in theater in New York City, and then moved to Los Angeles. After decades in Hollywood and many adventures, he moved to the country in Vermont, where he now lives with his wife, Barbara, and two beloved dogs, Willy and Zoey.

Printed in the United States
by Baker & Taylor Publisher Services